# VINA

## In the Eyes of a Child

By

K. S. Thomas

Edited by: Geo Dailey

This book is a work of non-fiction. Names and places have been changed to protect the privacy of all individuals. The events and situations are true.



ISBN: 1-4107-7360-4 (e-book)
ISBN: 1-4107-7359-0 (Paperback)

Library of Congress Control Number: 2003094970

This book is printed on acid free paper.

Printed in the United States of America
Bloomington, IN

1stBooks - rev. 09/18/03

# Contents

# Dedication

Dedicated to the memory of my beloved Daughter, Jennifer Renee. Whose untimely death prompted my search and the writing of this book: May she rest in God's graces.

# Acknowledgements

This book is my journey through life after I suffered the loss of my identity. It discloses many details that relate to the search for my family and those avenues that opened doorways to a new life.

In order to complete this book, the assistance of a number of people was both welcome and necessary. I would like to thank my three sons: Jeffery, James and Thomas. Without their support and understanding, this day would not have been possible.

I would also like to thank my birth and adopted siblings. Without their strong bonding, I would not have survived the early struggling years of abuse. Also, thank you for standing by me in the later years as we explored our past. Every page of that past that we opened created mountains of stress and caused pent-up pressures to erupt unexpectedly. I thank God that I did not have to endure those moments alone.

A special thank-you, to my adopted parents: Mr. and Mrs. Thomas. Without them, I would not have survived the trials and tribulations that arose in my lifetime. Armed with their love and support, I gained the confidence in myself to master the challenges set before me.

I would like to send a special thank-you to my birth sister Betty. We have endured so much pain in our lives together and I would not have had the strength to write this book without her love and support.

For his special contributions, which enabled me to spend the necessary time on the completion of this manuscript, my heartfelt thanks to Robert Gazso.

Last, but by no means least, are my dearest friends and conspirators, George and Marcia Dailey. Their contributions are too many to list but without whose guidance and generosity, I might not have been able to publish this book. Thank you both, once again!

# Preface

This is a story of my life as I remember the actual events. This book is not an attempt to embarrass or cause harm to any of the participants. For that reason many of the people in this story have had their names changed or omitted entirely.

Some portions of this book deal with sexual abuse, including child molestation, incest and bestiality. These sections are not meant for titillation, there was nothing exciting about what occurred. It was brutal degradation and against all laws both civil and moral.

It is my sincere hope that the publication of this book may help to ease the anguish others may be feeling, those who have suffered from similar circumstances. As for myself, this book serves a twofold purpose, the first being the closure of my nightmarish past and secondly the redemption of promises made to members of my families. My loved ones; both birth and adopted.

There are numerous mentions of supernatural events. These continue to make their presence known to me. I do not ask you to believe, but only to understand how they have influenced my life. I have made a journey back in time, a regression of sorts. As modern science has shown, even eyewitness accounts can be flawed. Any errors that may come to light are strictly unintentional and I ask your forgiveness.

I have been asked, “How did this happen? Why didn’t you seek help?” I can only state that even with all the safeguards that the Social Services are equipped with today, one has only to pick up a newspaper to read stories of child molestation, abuse and even death. In my book you will read of all the Red Flags that should have been seen by the professionals, my doctors, teachers and clergy. The malnutrition, the multiple bruises and signs of withdrawn behavior.

This occurred in the turbulent 1960’s. During that decade the United States was engulfed in an Asian war and the protests, which accompanied that conflict. We watched the inner cities erupt into violence as the Civil Rights movement struggled for acceptance. A child of six years, from a poor family was so easily overlooked. This book reads like a Charles Dickens' novel. The fact that it happened in this country in the closing decades of the twentieth century is a travesty.

# 1. Revelations

Fall 2002 I embarked on a journey in search of my family and my own identity. Back through the decades filled with abuse, despair, shame and humiliation. This quest brought back the horrors of my youth, the theft of my name and the dismantling of my family. The Clan as my birth mother called it.

My mother claimed Cherokee heritage from her father's side. My maternal grandfather was said never to have worn white men's clothing. This figure was to play an important role in my life. One saying, which I was to remember throughout my life, "look straight into the eyes, they mirror the soul," was more than once the only indicator of truth I was to know.

The Cherokee have a strong sense of family values. Many of their traditional beliefs and myths were to help explain those occurrences, which a young girl could have had no knowledge of. I researched some of the culture surrounding the afterlife; the presence of ghosts and the existence of the "little ones" believed to be the protectors of the young. They were protective not only of those in physical danger but also those in need emotionally. These beliefs made the acknowledgement of my grandfather's ghost and other visions much easier for me.

A Native American co-worker claims I have the visions or as the Irish and others of Celtic heritage call the "sight". Have the intermarriage of the cultures manifested this ability in me? I can only believe that it has. Too much that is supernatural has injected itself into my life. Many accused my mother of being a witch. Her physical appearance, vocal outbursts and other strange behavior did nothing to dispel these notions. The knowledge that the Cherokee practiced witchcraft and sorcery leaves me more a believer than one with doubts.

I was to continue on this path tracing the chain of cruelties perpetrated on my siblings and myself. The indifference of the legal system, which left my birth father, unpunished for his transgressions.

The callousness of those courts that stripped me of my birthright and then scattered my brothers and sister to the winds, now follow in the footsteps I have taken along my *trail of tears.*

December 1965, Flint, Michigan; I'm one of six children that resided in a small two-bedroom home with my family. My parents occupied one bedroom while my four brothers shared the other. My sister and I slept upon a sofa sleeper in the living room. Although small, it offered a place to lay my head. Every night was the same sleep was my enemy. Many nights, my eyes remained open, as sleep was difficult in coming. This night proved to be different. As I lay next to my sister on the small sofa, the room seemed strange, filled with a mysterious darkness in which sleep rapidly overtook me. To this day I cannot begin to explain what I was to experience that night. A dream unlike any other, a dream continuing to haunt me even today, in which I appear detached from my frail body. I am without hearing but I can see the small-darkened room, the furniture, a black and white television, that desk with a citizen band radio and that ancient lamp. Lost in a twilight zone between unconsciousness and wakefulness I began my journey.

My grandfather awakened me. Picking me up and sitting me upon his lap, he said he needed to talk to me. This was not uncommon for him. I loved my grandfather whom had a way of making things seem so peaceful. Sitting on his lap, I noticed that his eyes appeared so tired, He was showing signs of aging and like all old people, I thought he needed sleep. Why should he be an exception? Yet this time he seemed different, he was more comfortable, he was at peace with himself, as if a heavy burden had been lifted. This made me feel very secure in his arms.

Like any grandparent, he offered love and support. I felt safe in those strong arms, something that I did not take for granted. He held me tenderly as he looked out of the large picture window. There was definitely something different about him but I could not explain it. At first he rocked quietly, neither of us breaking the silence. I watched him as he rocked. His silver gray hair was neatly combed. I knew he had been sick, so the pale coloring that captured his face did not seem odd. Still, he looked different.

He was very dear to me and every moment I spent with him, I cherished. He sat in that favorite rocking chair with my body curled up on his lap. My long brown hair cascaded down his shoulder as I lay quietly in his arms, the faint aroma of tobacco smoke clinging to his sweater. The chair tilted back and forth as if rocking a baby. I looked around the room as he rocked me. It was a very comfortable room. His furniture matched, unlike the sofa and chair in my house. The colorful pictures upon the walls and the portraits of his family on his desk filled the room with a sense of warmth. I wished I could stay and live here in his house. His house was a home, offering plenty of love and support. That was something that did not exist in my house.

I am not sure how long we rocked in silence. But after a bit, he began to speak softly. He did not want to frighten me. So, he simply said that he had to go away and would not be coming back. Then suddenly he got up and walked to the window. I watched as he walked, his tall body strutting across the room as if he hadn't a care in the world. I had never seen him so relaxed. His eyes glowed as he looked out into the sky. Then, with the evening moonlight casting a glow upon his skin, for a moment I thought I could see right through him.

The tears started to fill my eyes. I wanted to go with him and I did not understand why he had to go away. As I watched him, the tears began to fall down my face. I did not want him to go. I was not sure how I could bear life without him. His visits brought peace to my life. But there was no point in discussing it his mind was made up. He was going to leave and my tears would not change that.

I started to get off the rocking chair but he motioned me to remain seated. As I slid back into the chair, it began to rock slowly of its own accord. Then, he said that he had something he needed to show me. It was something that would happen to me and he wanted me to know that when this occurred, I must remain strong. "You will not be alone. I will be there. Look for this sign," he said. Did this mean he was coming back? Was the sign going to be of him returning? As if my grandfather was reading my thoughts, he continued to say, "You will not see me then, but I will be there and somehow I will let you know."

The chair suddenly stop rocking and my heart started to beat heavily. Something was strange. The air became cooler and the room grew dark. There was a fine mist in the room. Grandfather was near but I could barely see him. It was as if he was disappearing. I was conscious but scared to death. I could just barely make out the room, as I watched his body float to my side. I saw him kneel beside me. I heard him whisper, “Watch carefully. Do not speak.” His voice seemed to echo as he said, “You will understand when the time comes. So just relax and watch.” My mind seemed to see images flashing around, but I felt safe, grandfather was there.

I felt free and weightless. It was as if I was floating, somehow defying gravity, leaving my body free to roam about the house. Each room filled with that foreboding mist, as if a dark shroud was covering the furniture. I thought am I, being carried by my grandfather? How else could I be traveling? As I floated into the living room, I suddenly became motionless. Looking down at the sofa bed, I saw my body resting on the pillow where I left it.

My body seemed to lose its weightlessness. The warmth of the blankets reclaimed my chilled body. Within a few seconds I turned to see my grandfather standing at the foot of the sofa bed. His voice, softened by the mist echoed quietly, “Remember, relax and watch, you will understand when you are older.” Then the vision appeared before my eyes. At first faint, then slowly an object materialized. White, a florescent, shimmering white slowly advancing, becoming larger as it approached. I thought it’s a house. Oh My God! It’s my house, now I could clearly see it. Then without warning, as slowly as it had appeared, the house vanished from my sight.

When I awakened, I felt well rested. I ran around the house looking for my grandfather. He was nowhere to be found. I stopped in the kitchen. My mother sat at the table staring off into space, as she often did for hours. I watched her, that long raven black hair strewn about her shoulders. The very picture of the witch, that the neighborhood children called her. Was she, casting spells upon the people? Was that why there was so much evil in my life? Am I, the daughter of a witch?

After several attempts at attracting her attention, she acknowledged me. I asked her where grandfather had gone? At first she acted like nothing was wrong and simply ignored the question. I continued to ask her about my grandfather. “Why,” she asked, looking somewhat surprised. “Because he was here last night and I want to know about the house,” I replied. My mother stared intently at me for what seemed like an eternity. It was unusual for her to give me this much attention. So, I told her about grandfather's visit and the talk we had the night before.

Mother laughed and said simply, "You must have been dreaming, your grandfather died last night." Startled, I blurted out, "Oh No! This, was not a dream, grandfather was here. I saw him. He rocked me in his rocking chair and showed me a sign." By this time my mother began to listen. She knew I was upset and had experienced something the night before. I stopped talking, my face turned ashen. I had realized that the rocking chair was at my grandfather's house. My mother, as if reading my thoughts softly whispered, "There is no way you could have gone to grandfather's house and returned last night. You were here all night." Now, I knew something was wrong.

Perhaps, if my birth mother had explained the beliefs of her father's people, I would have understood then, the quest that unfolded before me as my youth was torn from me. Instead, I feared the visions and questioned my sanity. Overtime I discovered the fact that my grandfather was Cherokee Indian. Although, he died when I was a small child, his presence guided me through the many years of torment after his death.

Now, after many years of research, the stories of spirit helpers and vision quests have helped me to understand that during my shattered youth, the spirit of my grandfather may have guided me. His spirit gave me the strength to overcome the challenges encountered as my *trail of tears* thrust itself upon me.

# 2. Forbidden Fruit

To an ordinary person that dream might seem frivolous. However, to a person that had given up on life by the age five, that dream would become my driving force for survival? It offered the hope that somehow my grandfather had understood the humiliation, the abuse and the pain I had suffered. Although the dream did not outline the chain of events to come, it presented the knowledge that through his death my grandfather's spirit would guide and protect me.

I know that at this point it sounds like I was crazy. In order to understand the full meaning of why I believe in the supernatural, you will have to know the secret I was forced to hide from society. I was born in the State of Michigan in 1960. My parents already had three boys, one girl and two other children that had died before I was born. So, I was the seventh child born to parents, which should never have had children.

In the early 1960's, we lived in a small upstairs apartment. By this time, I had another brother. My father had always voiced his opinion that females occupied a space beneath that of dogs. Men were created in the image of God; therefore females must obey his every command. Father considered himself the controller of life and death. Each day became one more test of survival.

It was not long before I would realize that I was put on this earth to pay for my sins. These sins that my father created, had instilled in me the belief that God himself had turned his back on me. Therefore, whatever happened to me was punishment that God himself had instructed my father to carryout.

One day, when I was approximately four years of age, I would realize the severity for not obeying his every command. It was in the afternoon hours and my older siblings were attending the local school. My parents had laid an old blanket on the living room floor. My father had instructed my mother and I to lie down upon it. To a four-year old child, that would be a good indication that it might be naptime. However, that was the furthest thing from my father's mind.

Sleep was not allowed, unless he himself had given permission. He was in charge of our every movement.

So I lay on the blanket beside my mother and father. At first, I turned to look away from my parents. I already feared my father and knew that my mother would not protect me, so my survival depended on my own abilities. I had already experienced beatings that left my body and mind paralyzed with fear. This time the pain my father forced upon my body would bring about a lifetime of terror. This time, he would show just how serious he was about having his every command obeyed.

Soon after laying on the blankets my parents undressed. I was instructed to watch as they had sexual intercourse. My father said that I needed to know why I was put on this earth. He had already shown my eight-year old sister sometime ago, now it was my turn. He informed me that I must watch them so I would know what to do. So I turned to face my parents. It wasn't long before I too, would participate in a mortal sin. I closed my eyes, not wanting to watch. That was not an option, I had not followed his every command, and I would have to learn to obey.

As I lay with tightly closed eyes, I felt a stinging slap across my face. Startled and shaken I opened my eyes. There on the floor my father pulled my clothes off me. In front of God and my mother, he forced my legs apart and entered savagely into me. My body thought it was being torn in two as each thrust left me gasping for breath. My only recourse was to dig my tiny nails into his skin. I must have scratched him for what seemed like hours. The harder I scratched, the harder he thrust himself into me.

Afterwards, I lay on the blanket; blood and semen oozing down my leg, praying that death would come quickly. My naked body shook from both fear and cold. Unable to move, I cried myself to sleep. However, sleep did not remove the pain. It only brought the reality of my punishment back. For now it was the only recourse I would have. There was nowhere to go; I would remain in this hellish life.

When I awoke my brothers and sister had returned home. Although I was clothed by this time, they sensed something was wrong. There they sat on the living room floor, wondering why I lay motionless. I looked into my sister's eyes; it was as if she knew.

Perhaps this was something she had experienced for years, while I had been unaware of the pain my father could cause.

I tried to move from the blanket, but my legs refused to co-operate. They remained in that spread position, just as they were a few hours before. Again, I tried to move them but the numbness remained. So I crawled across the floor to be near my older siblings. We huddled together and cried. My sister held me for hours as I cried, until the tears no longer fell.

Over the next couple of months, the sexual assaults continued. I no longer fought; it wasn't any use. It was happening, not only to me but also to the others. The five of us bonded, growing very close. Driven by hate for the father that robbed me of my innocence, I survived only for revenge. When our father went out with his friends, we all begged our mother for help. She would just look at a wall in the room or stare aimlessly into space. Leaving us with tear filled eyes and humiliated for resorting to begging for life itself.

One night after my father returned home drunk, there was a strange man screaming at him to come outside. There, at the bottom of the stairs stood a man with a gun. He was threatening to shoot our father. I know one of the commandants is that you should honor your mother and your father. I hoped God would forgive me because I prayed that man would enter the apartment and shoot my father dead.

That night we would learn something important. It became what I referred to as the line up to hell. Our father would make us line up according to age. The oldest boy first, all the way down to whomever was the youngest. At the beginning of the line stood our mother. Our father ordered us outside to the stairs. There the oldest was instructed to sit on the top step and the rest of us to take our places further down, according to our ages. Being the youngest, I sat at the bottom of the stairs on a cold night, with a strange man with a gun ready to shoot the man I now hated. Our father remained inside the apartment, aiming his gun out the window. It was our job to watch for the man threatening him. We were told to yell, when we saw that the stranger was in sight.

I saw the man approach the stairs. His body crouching low, almost crawling then he leveled his gun. Pointing the gun towards where my mother and the six of us sat. I looked directly into his eyes. I should have been terrified but I wasn't. The fear of what was inside the apartment was greater than the fear from outside. At that point I remember praying that God allow this man to shoot me. At least I would die with dignity and not at the hands of my depraved father.

I don't know if he ran off because he saw a woman and six children sitting on the stairs or if the drinks he consumed earlier had worn off. Whichever it was, our nightmare had not ended. Into the apartment we walked. There we remained in line and listened as father ranted about us failing him. It was our fault that the man had escaped uninjured, so now we must pay.

My mother was beaten first, then Allen and so on down the line. Slapping, hitting, raining punches upon our bodies till the wee hours of the morning. When he finished with one, he would start on the next. His strength never waned; over and over he beat us, leaving marks and bruises all over our bodies. When we were given permission to sleep, we crawled to our beds. There, we huddled closely, our sore, bruised bodies, waiting for the nightmare to continue.

Not long after that occurrence, we moved. We left our home in the middle of the night. Stealing away, as if we were running away from something or someone. Whether it was from debt or another unknown reason, we were going to a new home. A place he told me would change our life forever.

We moved to a small two-bedroom white colored house. As if it was yesterday, I remember looking at the house for the first time. My father carried my sleepy body and the rest of the family walked behind. My mother carried Tommy in her arms. As my father opened the door he said, "Vina, this house will be different. I will be a better daddy. I promise that it will stop; I will not hurt any of you again. I hope it is not too late for you to love me." God only knew, that I wanted to believe everything he said. I needed something to hold on to, a reason to live.

That night I lay on the sofa bed with my sister and I thought that God had answered my prayers. My father had actually sounded sincere. In my heart I wanted to believe him. Now we had a home with a yard to play in and maybe now, he would buy us toys to play with. We would become like the others in the neighborhood. I could almost have forgiven him for everything he had done to me. ALMOST! With that thought I fell fast asleep and slept soundly.

Normally I would lie there waiting for something to happen. That night I slept soundly for the first time in what seemed to be years.

The next morning I awoke well rested and eager to begin the day. I think I actually smiled. That too had been a forbidden thing. My father always thought it was a sign meaning we had done something wrong; therefore we were punished for smiling. This morning was different; there was a new house, a promise and hope for a new beginning.

Neither of my parents worked, so we received welfare support. I always thought my father couldn't work because he was crippled. An injury he said had happened during the war. He was a hero; at least that is how he told it. However, in my eyes, his child, he was no hero. He was a depraved man full of anger, one that would beat and rape his own children.

It was not long before I realized that one our father's drinking buddies lived down the road. So, everyday shortly after moving into our new home he went out drinking, just like before. The promise was forgotten and life was as it was before. Only now, it was taking a turn for the worse.

His drinking occurred more frequently and so did the beatings. Now with the house, he could even have his friends over. There, in the kitchen he would drink, often spending the family's grocery money on booze for his friends. His friends and the drink were more important than feeding his children. There were many days we went to bed starving.

One summer day my father decided that he would black top the entire yard. He said, "Only good kids could walk on grass," so we could not leave the boundaries of the asphalt. There we sat in a black top prison, watching other children run and play on the grass. Sometimes I imagined that I was one of them, without a care in the world. What would life be like then? What would it be like to be happy?

We sat outside so my father and friends could drink, party and eat the food we had in the house. I couldn't remember the last time I had eaten. I went to the back yard where some green grapes had grown along the fence. I didn't wash them, just picked them off the vine and ate them. I ate until my stomach could not handle another bite. At first I had devoured them, swallowing without chewing. I hadn't wanted to be caught eating without permission. Eating without our father's consent was forbidden but I hadn't eaten anything all day or the day before. After awhile I began eating more slowly, forgetting the price I would have to pay. I wanted to taste the food in my mouth, to savor each bite.

God! Did I get sick; my head was in the toilet that night, throwing up each grape I had consumed earlier, leaving behind the evidence of my disobedience. Behind me stood my father, watching me as I vomited. Then, before I could flush the toilet, he grabbed me by the hair, forcing my face into the vomit. I closed my mouth and my eyes as tightly as I could. He held my head in the bowl for a long time. Gasping for air, I heard him as he snarled, "Next time you disobey, God wants me to kill you." I had eaten of the *forbidden fruit* just like Adam and Eve and now even God would turn his back on me.

The next day we picked every grape on the vine. They were carefully placed into a brown paper bag and given to our father and his friends. My punishment was three days without food. I never forgot the sin of eating the forbidden fruit.

Even when my father's friends came over, the abuse did not stop. I think they actually enjoyed watching all of us being beaten. They watched and cheered my father on. Over time they became willing participants. They punched, slapped and pulled hair. We were some kind of animals meant only for their perverse enjoyment.

Soon I began to fear everything and everyone. My only escape was under the kitchen table. There I would lie for hours. Curled into a fetal position, watching for whomever might attack me. Even when they left, I would remain under the table. It was my haven, an escape from the world around me.

Under the kitchen table, there was a hole in the wall from which mice would enter and leave. I watched them run by my feet and along the wall near the stove. After sometime, they would come closer to me, sometimes stopping. Although they saw me, they never appeared to be afraid. I gave them names. Several times I imagined that they danced for me under the table. Even the mice in the house had a better life than I. They could find food and happiness. I found only misery!

When I thought everyone was gone, I would crawl out from under the table. Usually by this time it was bedtime. It didn't matter if I missed my bedtime; it wasn't like I was going to be told a story. My father would never read a bedtime story and my mother could not read us to sleep, since she had never learned to read or write.

During the summer of 1965, I begged my father to let me sit on the grass near the curb. I wanted to feel the grass with my bare toes. I wanted a taste of what the other kids in the neighborhood had. I wanted freedom, to go out from behind the fence. We never went anywhere. I felt caged like an animal, I always felt trapped.

For some reason, I actually got my own way. I could sit on the curb and because we lived on a corner, I could see people. Other people playing ball, riding bikes, and running down the road. My sister Betty had to watch me so we sat on the curb. We were free from the fence, observing the people around us. As we watched, everyone ignored us. Most of the neighbors thought of my mother as a witch, so everybody stayed away from our house.

My mother would go crazy now and then. Sometimes she would run naked down the street, her long black hair blowing in the wind, the only covering for her nakedness. My mother had her problems too! She was subjected to father's beatings and sexual abuse also. Sometimes, I thought she had enough.

So on the curb we sat, just as I had promised. I was told never to walk on the grass. I was so happy to be away from the house, I stood up and twirled around just like a ballerina. Up on my toes, as high as I could reach, I spun once and then twice. I was in heaven. Then momentarily, one foot landed on the grass. While trying to get my balance, I suddenly felt a sharp pain in my foot. A small piece of glass had sliced open my foot. Betty quickly carried me to the house. Into the kitchen she ran, screaming for help all the way. There stood our father, madder than hell! I had walked on the grass. Not only had I disobeyed, my actions had caused him to cancel plans with his girlfriend.

When we were in the car, he slapped my face so hard that I spit out a tooth. I hated every red light we stopped at, because each red light brought another round of slapping. When the doctor came into the office, I had completely forgotten about my foot. My mouth, face and all the rest of my body ached so much, that the pain in my foot was nothing.

He turned to my father and said he was concerned about all the bruises on my body. He said he had never seen so many marks on a body before. My father was prepared. He turned to the doctor and said, "She appears to be having trouble walking. Her feet turn in and she trips a lot. I have tried to find her good shoes to help her and I have scheduled an appointment with a foot doctor next week. She does need to have her feet corrected." After the doctor stitched my foot up, he told my father to reschedule the appointment he had for me because I could not walk on my foot all summer. Then he wrapped my foot and wrote something onto a chart.

After a few minutes, he looked at my father and asked how old I was. My father replied, "Five." The doctor then asked if I had received my school shot yet. Father said, "No." The doctor asked, "Are you sure? Just let me check her file." My father anxiously stated, "I'm sure she hasn't gotten her school shots yet. I'm in a hurry. Just give her the shot so we can get out of here." I prayed that the doctor had noticed his nervousness, and would remember that I had been in just a few weeks before to receive my shot. The doctor had commented then on my bruises also. Why didn't the doctor help me? Instead he pulled a large needle from one of the cabinets and gave me a shot in my arm.

I knew I had gotten my shot. But my father would have beaten me for talking to the doctor. So I hopped all the way to the car. I was not supposed to put any weight on my foot and my father refused to help me. When we got into the car, my father told me I would probably die before the day was over because I had gotten my shot a couple weeks before and it was deadly to receive two of them.

The next day I was told my punishment. For the rest of the summer, the rules of the house were as follows. All the males were to eat first. Of course, that was if there was food. Then mother and Betty followed by the dog and then I could have the scraps. Supper was to be our only meal, except those occasions when we received pancake mix from the welfare services. Bob, my eldest brother could make the best pancakes.

My father kept to his word. I ate last. There were many nights I went without. One night, I remember crawling to the dog's dish and eating his leftovers. My father stood there and watched as I ate after the dog. When I went to crawl to bed, he grabbed me, pulling me by the hair into the bathroom. I screamed in pain, as he forced his fingers into my mouth and down my throat. He raged, "You were told to eat last. That was the dog's food and he might have been hungry later." Our poor little doggie might get hungry, I really felt sorry for him! We remained in the bathroom until my father felt I had thrown up all the food I had eaten.

The next night, it was the same thing. There was no food for me. I needed to eat. Drifting in and out of consciousness, I saw my brother Allen, standing near the couch. In his pocket he had hidden some food. "Eat it fast," he whispered, "Father is outside and you won't get caught." One summer day a storm was brewing. The rain flooded our yard and the sky had turned that eerie shade of black. Our house had no basement, so when the weather turned bad, we would seek shelter in the pink house at the end of the block. An old lady lived there alone. Her husband had died in that basement just a few months before. The tornado sirens were blaring and out of the house we ran. Running to that basement for shelter. The winds were so strong that I could hardly run. The faster I tried to run, the less I could depend upon my feet. I was almost halfway there, when I tripped and fell into a ditch. While lying on the ground, I saw a small funnel cloud to the north of where I lay. There was no way I would yell for help. I would never endanger my brothers or sister.

I looked to see if the others had made it. They were all inside but my brother Allen, who was running towards me and yelling for me to get up. I could hear my father yelling, "Allen, leave her, she's not worth it!" So I stood up and ran as fast as I could. Then suddenly, I felt my brother grab and throw me into the ditch. There we lay, his body shielding mine. The funnel cloud never touched down and we were safe.

When fall arrived I started kindergarten. I was excited. I would be away from my father's sight. I could take a breath without feeling threatened. I remember my first day of school, as clearly as if it was yesterday. I wore a pretty white dress. Although it was my sister's old dress, it still looked pretty on me. I felt hopeful that I would find a friend and I would be able to play with someone my own age.

I slid on my only pair of shoes. They were the tennis shoes that three older children had worn out years before. I hated putting them on. They were full of holes and the broken laces could not be tied tightly enough. They were all I had but as I sat on the bed staring at my feet, my father said, "I saw the prettiest pair of shoes at the store yesterday. They did not cost a lot of money and I thought of the neighbors little girl. She would look pretty in those shoes but her feet are bigger than yours Vina, and they only had your size. So, I didn't buy them."

When I arrived at school. The teacher took attendance. She allowed us to play with the toys on the shelf. I played with the other boys and girls. I was normal. I laughed and smiled just like they did. When it was time to leave, I did not want to go. I could have stayed there for hours. I ran to the shelf, to put back the toy I had been playing with. I knew better than to keep my father waiting. My feet did not co-operate, tripping over my feet was normal for me. Down I went, knocking over the shelf and all the toys, making the loudest noise as I landed on the floor. In front of the entire class, I had made a fool of myself. I hated my feet.

Instead of comforting me, my father laughed the loudest. He of all people should have understood. He was crippled from the war. People must have made fun of him. Why wouldn't he take the time to explain to me, why my feet were different? Maybe a doctor could have helped me but father would never spend money on me to correct my feet.

All the way home my father laughed about the accident my feet had caused at school. "If only, I had better shoes, then my feet wouldn't turn in," I yelled. There in the driveway we sat in the car. I had known better than to yell and now I must pay. My father grabbed the back of my head and pulled my hair as hard as he could. Then slamming my head against the dashboard repeatedly until I promised never to raise my voice again.

After arriving home, I crawled to my place of safety under the kitchen with the mice. There I stayed until it was time for bed. There was no food for the family that night and only coffee to drink if you were thirsty. Welfare furnished us with powdered milk on occasion but I hated its taste. Therefore it was coffee or water. No wonder we were so sickly.

The next day at school, everyone laughed at my feet. The teacher tried to stop them but even she laughed on occasions too! So, under one of the tables I went and I refused to come out. The teacher had to call my father and I wouldn't come out for him either. Finally he dragged me out from under the table, I screamed and begged to be left alone. I wanted to hide from everyone who made fun of me. Now, even at school I was ridiculed. Under a table was my only safe haven.

My father was angry that he had to get me from school but this time I was not beaten. He never said a word in fact. After the older kids got home, my father explained to them what had happened and they told him I could attend they same school they went to. So my father had me transferred to the main school. Although other kids still made fun of my feet, I could at least walk to school with my family. I loved it.

Winter was always hard on us, our coats were threadbare and we did not have any boots. We had to walk to and from school, which also included a trip home at lunchtime. We had no hot lunch waiting for us, just the freezing cold. With our chilled bodies and empty stomachs we attempted to learn our lessons.

One day at school, the teacher pulled me aside and asked why I had so many bruises. I lied. I told my teacher that we lived in a two-story house and I fell down the stairs a lot because of my feet. The next day, the teacher pulled me aside again and said that she had driven by my house. It was a single story home. She proceeded to call my father and requested to speak with him in the office. I was terrified because my father always said he would kill us if we ever told.

When my father arrived at school, he told my teacher that I fell all the time because of my feet. I also heard my father say, "When I get a job, I will take her to get braces on her feet but for now she has to turn her feet in to get around." The teacher believed him. Just as he said she would! I knew the teacher had meant well but there was no escape for us. My father was prepared for anything they asked him and we knew that we would not be believed.

When we got home my father was furious. He dragged me into the house and he beat me with a belt until I could not sit. Then he went out with his friends. He came home after everyone had gone to bed. He woke everyone up and belted all of us. The usual lineup occurred, with him continuing the beatings.

The next morning when he woke me up, I was told to go into the boy's room. There he took a rope and tied it tightly around my throat. He was going to hang me for telling the teacher. I fought him with all my strength. My brother Allen tried to help me. He convinced my father that Social Services would investigate and that he should let me be. My father loosened the rope and let me out of thc closet.

The next day there were too many bruises for me to go to school so I got to stay home. Something most kids would have enjoyed. I hated staying home. He didn't hit any of us for the next couple of days. All our bruises would fade and disappear. After that, if he left too many bruises we stayed home. Sexual abuse however, did not leave any noticeable scars, so he never stopped that manner of abuse. That became an everyday event in our household. My body was his whenever he felt the desire.

The incident at school made me realize that there would be no escape. My only way out was to take matters into my own hands. I became suicidal. I had it all planned I would slice my throat. It was the easiest. My only escape now, was to end my life by my own hands. I had no desire to live.

I stood in the kitchen with the knife to my throat. Then, I saw ~~him watching me. With a demonic smile on his face, he turned to me~~ and sneered, "Go ahead! Do it! I never wanted you anyway!" My death, it seemed would give him satisfaction. There was no dignity in begging for my life or taking my own life. I decided then, that I would kill myself when he was away. I would not give him the satisfaction of watching me commit suicide.

I had completely given up on life. With nothing to hold onto, I prayed that God would strike me with a sudden illness. By the age of five, I had been beaten, starved, raped and hanged by my father. Was there a God that could just stand by and watch this? God must not exist! I was truly alone. That was December of 1965. The night my grandfather died. That night I saw my salvation, in a vision of the future to come.

# 3. Never Again

One of the most memorable things I learned in kindergarten was the meaning of Christmas. I learned that a man named Santa Claus came on Christmas Eve, bringing toys for all the good girls and boys. I had never heard of this before. I never knew that such a thing, as a holiday even existed. I listened intently as the teacher described how Santa came down the chimney, bringing gifts to hide under the Christmas tree.

Walking home that day, I noticed that every house I passed had a Christmas tree decorated with balls and lights; that were shining from their windows. I asked my brother Allen, why we never had a Christmas tree but he just shrugged his shoulders. I knew we were poor but surely a small tree wouldn't cost too much money. I just knew if we had a Christmas tree that Santa Claus would come. If he only brought just one toy for each of us, we would all have something to play with. When I got home I asked Betty and Bob about a Christmas tree. "Why can't we have one?" I cried.

So that night they took an old Sears' catalog and folded all of it's corners. Each corner was folded to a point. They had fashioned a homemade Christmas tree. Then, my brother Tommy and I took out our school crayons and colored each page green. We decorated the paper branches with balls colored red, yellow and blue. We had our first Christmas tree I knew Santa would come. I was sure that Santa Claus stopped at all the houses that had Christmas trees. I was so proud of that tree. I normally colored poorly but this tree was as nice as the others, in the homes I had seen.

That night I said my prayers and prayed that Santa would see our tree. Before I drifted off to sleep I heard my father come home. There he stood, in a drunken state, looking at my tree. It wasn't in his way. We had placed it by the window. He grabbed it and demanded to know what the hell it was and why it was in his house? Then he had all of us line up. There we stood in the living room as he lit the match. I looked into his anger filled eyes as he set the tree ablaze. All I could do was watch the tree turn to ashes and listen to my father scream at the top of his lungs. Slurring each word as he said, "There will be no Christmas in *HIS* house *EVER!* Christmas was for *GOOD* boys and girls. There are no good children here!" My tree was gone in minutes. My hopes of Christmas shattered.

That night as I lay in bed crying, Betty told me that Santa wasn't coming. It was only a belief that some people had. Santa really didn't exist. There was no holiday for us. We had never celebrated any holiday before, so why should this one be different. My father's words echoed through my mind all night long. He had yelled, "There will never be a Christmas in my house!" And there never was.

Christmas day was like any other day. We had no dinner, we received no new toys and we had no relatives to celebrate with. We did not even have a television to watch the parade. The outside world was closed off to us our only outside interaction, existed at school and we were not accepted there. The other children made fun of our clothes and the fact that we were the only white kids there. That coupled with the behavior problems we exhibited caused a lot of stressful times.

Even had we developed a friendship with another kid, they would not have been allowed to come over. Nor would we have been allowed to go to their houses. We were restricted to our prison. All we had were each other. When you are isolated from a normal life, you really don't miss what you never knew existed. So up until I started kindergarten, I never missed Christmas. They say ignorance is bliss and in my case they were right.

Christmas soon passed and school had started. Almost every kid in the classroom had a new outfit on. Everyone dressed in their Sunday best, showing off their Christmas outfits. I hated them! There I sat in the rags, wearing the welfare handouts that Betty had worn a few years before. I was small for my age, so most of my clothes were too big on me. I was the smallest kid in the classroom. My teacher had told me I needed to eat more because I wasn't any bigger than a two year old.

That day our assignment was to stand up and tell everyone what we got for Christmas. Each kid stood up and told what they had received. Everyone had a list of what their parents had given them and then what Santa had brought. When I stood up all the kids laughed.

"She's too poor. I bet she didn't get anything for Christmas," they yelled. Their words pierced me like a knife in the heart. I couldn't let them know the truth of their words. I stood there and I lied. I told them I had gotten two presents from my parents and that Santa had brought five more. I named off several toys that the other girls had mentioned. Although I had no idea what some of them actually were I had at least been able to convince them, that I had a Christmas.

Then came the hard part. The teacher said we could bring one of our new toys into school for Show and Tell. I was devastated! How could I bring in a toy I did not have? There was no way I was going to tell the class I had just lied. I waited until after class and I approached my teacher. I told her that Christmas wasn't celebrated at my house and I did not get any new toys to bring to the Show and Tell. I told her I had lied. With tears falling down her face, my teacher sadly said, "It was alright to tell a white lie this time because the other children had goaded you into it."

The next day the teacher explained to the class that each of us would have an assigned day to bring in their new toy. When my day arrived, she brought in a toy she had purchased for her daughter. I got to pretend it was my gift. So up in front of the class, I told another lie. Of course, this time it was with the teacher's blessing and co-operation.

As time progressed, so did the abuse. Many nights I lay awake watching my father drag one of my brothers from their bedroom into my parent's room. I would sneak closer to the door to watch. There in the bedroom my brother would be forced to have sexual intercourse with my mother. My father observing and instructing them in the acts he wanted them to perform. Afterwards, my brother was allowed to leave the room and return to his bed. Now, everyone in the household was subjected to my father's sick sexual obsessions.

He had control of both our physical and mental being. All six of us were beginning to exhibit emotional problems. One of my brothers was compulsively sucking his thumb. Two older brothers displayed hostility toward others, constantly getting in fights with the other children. I would hide under any object I could find; most of the time it was a table. All of us had numerous bruises covering our bodies. All the signs of an abusive environment were demonstrated but instead of receiving help and support we were ridiculed. We were outcasts in the neighborhood, at school and in our very own home. There were no means to release the pent up tensions, so we simply buried our hurt deep within us.

As spring approached, so did the birth of another child to our dysfunctional home. That was just what we needed, someone else to share in our misery. On the kitchen floor, my three-year old brother Tommy and I sat waiting for the new arrival. My mother lay on the bed in my brother's room, screaming in agony. I could hear my father's voice shrieking, "Hurry up, push this kid out. I have things to do bitch!" There was no compassion in his voice. His words were harsh and uncaring. I swear that he actually slapped her a few times for interfering with his plans.

It wasn't long before I could hear my mother's shrill voice begging, "The baby's coming. God! Get me a doctor! Please get me a doctor." At that point I could hear my father talking to the other man in the room. He was one of my father's best friends and he often came to the house. They were discussing whether to call for an ambulance. My father thought the two of them could deliver the baby and did not want anyone else in the house. His friend Jerry felt she needed medical attention and did not want to assist in the birth of a stillborn child. Reluctantly, my father called for an ambulance.

I watched as the ambulance drove up to the house. One of the medical attendants stood by the door and asked me if I wanted a brother or a sister? But before I could reply, I heard the other attendant yell, "The baby's head is out. Push as hard as you can."

I prayed for a sister. I wanted a younger sister to play with. Tommy already had three brothers. Yet, when the new baby boy arrived, I was glad it wasn't another girl. At what age, would my father start sexually abusing her? Maybe fate had intervened. Although Leonard would be subjected to the brutal beatings, he would be spared the sexual abuse, at least for a while.

With the birth of Leonard, there were now seven children in this house of misery. We vowed to protect him and shield him from the abuse. I remember Betty taking care of him, just as if he was her very own. From changing his diapers, to clothing his naked body, Betty watched over him continually. Now, Leonard was one of us. He was in our tribe. He became our responsibility at all times. We gave him a nickname, he was known as Chiefy, from that day forward.

Summer soon arrived and we acquired new neighbors. They had two children, a little boy about three and a little girl a year younger than I. Her name was Cathy. She was the happiest kid I knew. She never made fun of me. Accepting me for whom I was. I would sit by the fence and talk to her. When my father wasn't around we would talk for hours. We could never play together because I was not allowed to go next door nor was she allowed to come over. But she was my best friend, matter of fact she was my only friend.

I told Cathy about everything that happened in my house. She did not understand some of it but she knew my father beat me. The bruises were hard to hide. We always stopped talking whenever my father approached. I knew better than to let him hear me talking about the "secrets of the house." Talking to Cathy allowed me to let out some of the pain I held inside me. I had never told anyone before, I was always too terrified that I would get caught. My father always told me that he would kill me if I told. So, I had to keep it a secret. I kept the pain buried deep inside. Cathy was my only outlet.

We were best friends that entire summer. Soon school started and I attended the main school all day. Cathy could have attended the same school but her mother chose to have her attend kindergarten at one of the satellite locations. Therefore, we could not walk to and from school together. When we arrived home we would sit by the fence and talk to each other. Cathy had a loving, happy family. Her father worked hard to support them and her mother took care of her and her younger brother. She had everything a little girl could want but I was not jealous of her, I cherished her friendship. She was my only outside contact that treated me as a human being.

One day in the early fall Cathy showed me a magazine. It had pictures of all kinds of dolls. Her mom told her to pick out the doll of her choice as a birthday present. God! Was she a lucky girl? She asked me to help her pick out her doll. On my side of the fence, I sat looking at all those pretty dolls, wishing I could have one. When Cathy left to go in for dinner, I heard footsteps, so I quickly tucked the magazine inside my shirt and went inside.

I must have looked at that book one hundred times. I dreamed of having a doll to play with. There was one doll I liked the best. She had the prettiest smile on her face. I loved that smile. After my father had left to go drinking, I went into the kitchen and got the scissors. I carefully cut out the picture of that doll. Surely, Cathy would not notice what I had done. There were other dolls to choose from and that picture had been at the end of the book.

The next day after school, I gave Cathy her magazine back. As we sat by the fence, I told her about my father's friend Jerry. He was watching me when I undressed. Every night by the window, I saw him staring at me. I had no other place to change and every night for the past two weeks there he stood. Then last night, he walked through my door while I was changing. I tried to cover myself with my nightclothes but he pulled them away from my body. There I stood naked, helpless and humiliated. There was nowhere to hide and nobody to help me.

He slowly looked at every inch of my naked body, then after a few minutes he turned and walked away. I quickly dressed and ran for the table. There I lay in my safe haven until the wee hours of the morning. My body shook with fear and the cold as the dampness of the kitchen floor revived me. I quietly ran to the sofa bed and covered my chilled body with the thin blanket I shared with my sister. There I lay, staring at the front window, wondering if he would return to use my body for his sexual desires.

As I spoke, Cathy looked puzzled? She had no idea what I was talking about. She understood the beatings and the lack of food but she had no clue about what sex was or why a man wanted to watch you undress. She yelled aloud, "I don't understand what you are taking about! Why would a man do that? You are only a kid, just six years old! Did you tell your father?"

There at the edge of the fence stood my father, listening to every word we had said. I knew I was dead. There was no way I could escape from this. He had heard our conversation. "Get in the house right now, VINA!" he bellowed. I ran as fast as my feet would take me. I ran to the table. I shook with fear as the door slammed behind him. There he stood beside the table, demanding that I come out. My legs were numb with fear, I couldn't move. In a voice, I had never heard before, he screamed, "If you don't get the hell out from under that table, I will go get that little girl and I will kill her! Then her death will be your fault!"

I crawled to the edge of the table and slowly stood up. Knowing I was dead anyway, I yelled, "Go ahead, kill me. At least I won't have to live like this!" I looked straight into his eyes as I spoke. At first he didn't hit me, he just stood there madder than hell. Then he grabbed my frail body and began shaking me severely. He raged on saying, "Little girls are just deformed babies. They never should be allowed to live. Females are put on earth just for one thing and one thing only. Should I have every man in the neighborhood do that to you?"

He slapped me across the face, leaving a stinging sensation and his handprint on my cheek. What scared me more was the demonic look in his eyes. I knew he was not through with me. When I least expected it, he would finish what he started today. I would have to be on guard at all times.

The next day after school, I saw Cathy at the corner. She stood there looking at me and I could tell by the look in her eyes that she was mad at me. She had found where I had cut out the picture of the doll and would not speak to me. She just threw the magazine at me. I had lost my best friend and I was heart broken.

Of course my father stood there by the door waiting for me to come home. He wasn't watching to make sure I made it home safely. He was making sure I was not talking to Cathy. So, into the house I went, I crawled under the table and remained there the rest of the day. I wanted my father to leave, and then I could take the picture to Cathy and apologize. But! He never left.

The evening was quiet. There were no beatings, just an eerie kind of silence throughout the house. It was as if he was waiting for something. Perhaps he thought Cathy's family had turned him in. We even ate dinner that night, my mother's famous bean soup. My father and a couple of the older children had walked to the store. He had to walk or get a ride with his friends because somehow he had lost the family car. He purchased a few items and asked the butcher for a ham bone for his dog. The butcher didn't charge him anything for the bone and mother used it to flavor the soup.

The next day after school, Cathy was at the other corner waiting to cross. I did not see my father. I thought if I hurried I could catch her and apologize. She was standing there, motioning a woman in a station wagon through the intersection. The driver hesitated and signaled Cathy to go ahead. After they both had motioned to each other a couple times, they both moved at once. I heard the shrieking of the tires and then Cathy's scream! My brother grabbed me and held me tightly so I couldn't see. I did not have to see to know that Cathy had been hit. Her scream and the thumping sound as her head hit the car, told me that Cathy had been hurt. I wanted to run to her but my brother would not let go. I struggled to free myself but he held me firmly in his grip. I could just barely make out the words he spoke, "Oh God! Vina, don't look at Cathy." He continued to speak, "Vina, Cathy has been hit."

"God let Cathy live," I pleaded. I saw the woman who had hit her. She was a young woman that had just picked up her little daughter from school. She was kneeling on the curb crying and screaming for someone to help Cathy but nobody knew what to do. The ambulance arrived and with sirens blaring, took Cathy to the hospital.

That night when my father came home, I heard my mother tell him about Cathy. He came straight to the sofa bed and whispered quietly, so Betty wouldn't hear, "I told you not to say anything to anyone and now look what you've done. You killed Cathy! God saw to it that you were punished. Poor Cathy had to pay for your sins. I told you nobody would ever believe you. See! I was right!"

Cathy's father stopped by the next day. He told my mother that Cathy had made it through the night but she had a lot of tubes in her. She was in very serious condition and was not expected to make it. I begged to go see her. Her father turned and hugged me tenderly. He spoke softly, tears falling from his eyes, "The doctor will only allow the immediate family and even we cannot stay long. I think it is best that you don't see her this way."

The next day, Cathy's father came by again. I lay quietly under the table as he said to my father, "Take care of the little girl you have. I just lost mine. I see bruises on your children and I hear the screaming coming from your house. If, I see another bruise on that child, I'll turn you into to Social Services." My father became furious. I saw punch after punch land on Cathy's father's face. He finally retreated, bloody and beaten the only person, who had tried to save me, had failed. I was doomed, trapped in this life of hell.

Soon after the fight, Cathy's family moved and I never saw them again. I should never have told anybody. If I had kept silent,

Cathy would still be alive and her father would never have been hurt. I swore that somehow I would let her know how sorry I was.

Shortly after the death of Cathy, my uncle from out of town arrived. My father sent all of us children outside. While we sat on the asphalt wondering what to do, some suggested we hold a séance. I didn't know what a séance was but my cousin explained that at a séance you brought somebody back from the dead, to ask that person about something. Immediately, I wanted to bring back Cathy. We sat there on the asphalt, holding hands, concentrating. I closed my eyes and prayed that God would let me have this chance to apologize. At first, nothing appeared to happen. Then after a few moments, I opened my eyes and stared into the night sky. In between the stars, was a white object, I was not sure what it might be but it scared me half to death. I yelled, "I am sorry Cathy!"

In my heart I had fulfilled a promise. Cathy had somehow known that I was sorry for everything. I am not sure how I knew but I just did. At that moment I vowed never to endanger another living soul. I promised never to tell the *secrets of the household.*

# 4. Dark Ages

Cathy's death left me all alone. I was isolated from the real world and had lost the will to live. I had made numerous attempts at suicide and failed. With no recourse available, I now spent most of my time after school, under the table. There, I watched the mice scamper to and from the kitchen, as I hid from everything and everybody.

One evening, while I laid in bed, a mouse crawled up onto my shoulder. I was terrified. Although I had watched them for hours under the table, I never had one crawl on me before. I lay very still praying it would go away. My father came in to the room and very quietly said, "If he bites you, you will die." He offered no help, just simply walked away. Soon the mouse crawled off my bed. I lay there for hours wondering why I was not afraid of them while I was under the table but terrified of them when away from my safe haven?

My father and his friend Jerry went out almost every night. My father had purchased a citizens band radio some time ago and Jerry had a mobile unit in his car. They claimed to drive around at night and radio the police when they found strangers that needed help. Although, neither of them had any medical knowledge, they felt that the neighborhood was a safer place because of their patrols.

Each night my father came home late and drunk. Most of the nights he just went to bed. Then there were those nights, when he woke everyone up for a round of beatings. Afterwards, describing how he became the hero of the night, having saved somebody's life. Still, I could not picture him as a hero.

The fighting between my mother and father began to worsen. Everyone in the house would lay and watch the fistfights, which erupted. After my father beat her, my mother would sit at the table and gaze into space. Then he would take his anger out on us. Each of us taking our place in line as he worked off his rage and frustration. Their marriage problems stemmed from the abuse and another woman. On the weekends, everyone in the house could hear my father talking to his girlfriend over his CB radio. His conversations were coarse and graphic and I knew my mother was aware of his indiscretions. Although she chose to stay with him, the other woman remained a constant threat to their marriage. I remember one night that my parents fought over the other woman. My father had told her that she could sleep with whomever she wanted to. That night a couple of my father's friends stopped over and the night took an ugly turn. My father informed her that she could sleep with any of his friends. As my mother ran into the living room, my father grabbed her and dragged her back into the kitchen. At first my mother resisted, I watched as my father and another man held her down as the third started slapping her when she screamed for help. There was no stopping them; they raped her numerous times. This lasted for hours; afterwards my mother lay on the floor in a fetal position, crying throughout the night.

I had wanted to go to her but I could not leave my safe haven. I had fallen to sleep hours before and awakened when father and his friends came home. All I could do was watch. I feared for my mother and I feared they would discover me. So I remained under the table with the mice until the morning hours.

The next night as my father was going out, I heard him tell my mother that it was all right for him to see his girlfriend because she had slept with some of his friends last night. As my father walked out the door, I could see the fire in my mother's eyes. Still, she would not leave him. She swore that she loved him and no matter what he had done, she would always stand by him.

It wasn't long afterwards, that the tension between the blacks and whites, became a concern to the neighborhood. Even on the school grounds, the tensions were building. My father decided that it was no longer safe for Tommy and I to walk home alone. He forced my older brother Allen to drop out of high school. Allen was to walk the two of us to and from school. My father had given him a walkie-talkie to contact home, if an emergency arose. One day while walking home, a little black boy hit me on the back of my head with a bottle. Because the boy was so much younger than he was, my brother just yelled at him. As we walked away, the little boy yelled that he was going to get his big brother.

Within minutes a crowd had gathered. It appeared to us that at least fifty blacks were chasing us. Despite my poor feet, we ran as fast as we could. The street we normally took home was the scene of a lot of fighting. My brother decided it would be safer to take the longer way home. Picking up Tommy and I, he carried us away as fast as he could. Seeing the mob was gaining on him, he stopped long enough to radio our father. At first my father did not respond, so Allen kept trying to radio him. After several attempts my father answered. He told Allen that he was busy talking to his girlfriend and that he was not to lead the blacks home.

Allen threw the walkie-talkie across the street, shattering it into pieces. Picking Tommy and I up once more, he ran as fast as he could. When we finally reached our home, we found the doors had been locked. We knocked on the door but there was no answer at first. After numerous attempts of knocking, my father yelled, "Keep the blacks away from me and your mother."

Allen hid my brother and me in the doghouse. Unprotected, he waited outside, watching for my other brothers and sister to come home. Bob, Betty and James rode the school bus, when the bus arrived you could see that fighting was going on. I heard screams coming from the back of the bus. It was Betty! She was trapped at the back of the bus. We watch in horror as my brother Bob fought his way to the back of the bus. Allen tried to get on the bus but the driver refused to let him on. My brothers and sister were finally able to leave the bus, James had received a bloody nose, my brother Bob, had been sliced across the throat with a knife. Although not very deep it had bled a lot. Betty had been beaten up and her clothes had been torn, luckily she had not been raped.

After they got off the bus, my father still refused to let us into the house. We remained outside until after dark and he felt it was safe enough to open the door. He offered no help in attending our wounds. We had to take care of each other. My brother Bob never got stitches, the scar on his throat remained for a long time.

The tension between the blacks and whites lasted for a while and we tried to stay clear of the fighting. My brother Bob tried to explain to me why they were rioting. He said, "They are fighting for equal rights. Many years ago they had to fight for freedom. They want to be treated as human beings." Although I was only seven years old at the time, I understood exactly how they felt. My family was never targeted again; perhaps they realized that we had our own problems. The rest of the whites in the neighborhood continued to have problems however, as the rioting continued to run its course. We did not become victims of the blacks, only those of our demented father.

Over the next couple of months, my mother showed signs of another pregnancy. As her stomach grew, she became greatly depressed. Horrified, I watch her beat on her stomach trying to induce a miscarriage. This went on for sometime until one day when she started hemorrhaging. When the blood started pouring down her leg, she began to panic. My father laid her in one of the boy's bed and he forced Betty to take care of her. Although Betty was only eleven or twelve years old, my father felt that she was capable of dealing with that medical crisis. Betty began to panic and cry, within a few minutes she yelled, "She is going to die if you don't get her to a hospital!" Reluctantly, my father called an ambulance.

John Calvin was delivered a short time later. He was born with numerous birth defects and his struggle for life was a short one. I never saw John Calvin but mother said he had one of his legs where an arm should have been. His funeral was small, only my parents and the seven of us children attended. I remember standing in the cemetery as they brought the tiny casket to the gravesite. I had never seen such a small casket. My bothers Bob and Allen wanted to see what the baby looked like. I just stood there praying that God would take care of our new baby brother better than his parents would have, had he survived.

Shortly after the death of John Calvin, my mother had to have surgery. She came home with numerous stitches in her stomach. After a fight between my parents, some of the stitches tore loose. As she lay on the kitchen floor with her stomach hanging out, my father refused to call an ambulance. This time however, within minutes Betty called for medical assistance. My mother recovered but I realized then, that my father would hide his abuse at any cost even if it meant the lives of his family.

As the months progressed, our father's drinking became even more excessive. We were living on welfare, so money was always tight. He needed more money to purchase his booze. He decided that all of us kids except Chiefy, who was the youngest, could leave our fenced blacktop and search the streets. He had given us permission to look for money. We were not to come home until we found enough for him to go drinking with.

I remember looking back at the house as I walked away. I had started to run at first, and then I realized I could not leave Chiefy alone with that horrible man. So, I turned around and walked back to my boundary. As I walked, the house glowed. It became larger at first and then smaller. It repeatedly changed its size, again and again. I stood in the street watching that damn house glowing and changing size. What was wrong with me? I had convinced myself that I was crazy two years ago when I heard my grandfather speaking from the dead. After all, nothing had happened then surely grandfather would not just stand by and allow his own blood to live like this.

My mother told me several times how he tried to protect us when he was alive. He had nicknamed me, his little papoose, when I had almost died with pneumonia at six months old. Apparently, my father decided to lay me down on the porch so he could drink with his friends in peace and quiet. Although it had begun to storm, I was left out in the rain screaming. Several hours later, my grandfather stopped by to check on us and rushed me to the hospital. I was diagnosed with double pneumonia and the doctors did not think I would survive. My grandfather and father fought for months because of this. They would never reconcile over this incident.

I had not had another vision in two years nor did I think grandfather was with me. After all, ghosts don't really exist, do they? At least not those ghosts which would protect me. The thought of that dream scared me. I feared the vision because it seemed to be just another way to torment me. Why would anyone come back from the dead to rescue somebody? Why should it take this long? There had been plenty of time to strike my father dead. OH! He would come back to haunt me. If anybody could, he would, he'd find a way. There was no escaping, there was no way out, just ask him.

Suddenly, I heard a car blowing it's horn for me to move. Slowly, I moved out of the way. I don't remember how long I had stood there thinking of the house and grandfather. I had blocked that dream from my memory a long time ago. Down the road I went, looking for money. It wasn't long before I heard someone calling my name. I turned around, there stood a man. He spoke softly, "Vina, I am here. Don't be scared. Hold on to the vision I have shown you. You'll need it from here on out; soon you'll be free. Don't give up, my little papoose." Then he disappeared before my eyes.

I walked around for a while and found a few quarters. There, at the end of the block, I could see my family walking home. Allen had found a five-dollar bill. Between the others we had found enough money for my father to go out. On the way home we debated whether or not to tell father about the five-dollar bill. We gave father everything but the paper money. Then Allen showed him the bill and asked if Bob and him could walk to the store and buy some food. My father ripped the money from Allen's hand and out the door he went. Needless to say of course, no food was bought for us.

When my father went out, I sat on the couch, wondering what that man, my grandfather meant? "I'll need it," he had said. What could be worse than what I was already going through? Jerry was still watching me undress at night, my father still made me have sex with him and the amount of food I had to eat barely kept me alive. What else could happen to me, that was so bad, that suddenly my grandfather's ghost would show up?

Over the next couple of months the abuse worsened. My father had to be in total control of everything. Every Sunday morning the seven of us went to church. My father and mother never attended. There we sat praying for the forgiveness of our sins. I was totally convinced that if there was a God, he hated me. One Sunday as I sat praying, the minister came over and say down beside me. He asked how I had gotten two black eyes and all the bruises on my body? I told him, "I couldn't tell, that it was a secret." The minister responded, "If you tell God, he will help you." I quickly replied, "I promised never to endanger anyone again. God already knows what is happening and he allows it to happen!" The minister was somewhat surprised by my response and quickly replied, "God doesn't give you more than you can handle, my child." In a voice older than my years, I answered, "Tell your God, I am only seven years old."

The next Sunday, I decided I would stay home. Although father usually forced us to go to church, he allowed me to stay home. So I stayed in bed while all the others left for church. By this time, I shared a room with my mother and my sister. When the others had left, my father said that I had sinned by not going to church and God would punish me. I just felt like staying home and watching the old black and white television my father had picked up at a garage sale. This time I had gotten what I wanted. Why?

It wasn't long before I heard Jerry's voice. I prayed he would go away but my father invited him in for coffee. There I lay with my nightclothes on, regretting not going to church. It wasn't long before the bedroom door opened and there he stood. Staring at me as he had done before. I screamed, "Leave me alone!" He wasn't touching me, just watching me. I could not stand the look in his eyes, I knew what he was thinking and there was no one there to help me. A few moments after Jerry had entered the room, he closed the door behind him. There I stood helpless, terrified, petrified with fear unable to move. I opened my mouth to scream but nothing came out. He grabbed me, threw me upon the bed and raped me.

The next thing I remember, was waking up and feeling dirty. I ran for the bathroom and scrubbed my body. I felt so filthy. I lay in the bathtub, soaking my sore, bruised body for more than an hour. Afterwards, my mother came in and gave me some aspirin. Somehow, I had received a blow to my head during the struggle. My father only laughed and said I didn't deserve anything for the pain. I looked around to see where father's friend was because I did not to be anywhere near him. My father saw me look and said with a wicked grin, "Jerry's left. He's had what he wanted!" I went to my bedroom to make my bed and I noticed blood on the sheets. I stripped the bed as I cried.

Every night after that, sleep was my enemy. The same nightmare haunted me for months. Jerry's eyes watching me, his hands touching me, raping me, just as my father had. I had only my Grandfather's words to comfort me. That vision was my only sanity. It was my only solace; I would cling to that memory every night, wondering if tomorrow would lead me to a day of salvation. Yet each day was the same, another day in Hell!

By the time I turned eight, I had nearly given up all hope of escape. I was not the only one looking for an escape, all of us were. Allen was now sixteen and somehow had managed to save enough money to buy two old cars. He thought that if Bob and him, could get just one of them running, they could drive us far away. We decided we could live in tents, just as our grandfather did.

The car became our hiding place. When our father came home drunk during the daylight hours, we all hid in the car or anywhere else we could find. The physical abuse remained constant. Our teachers questioned the bruises but only Betty's teacher sent a note for my father to come to the school. When my father returned home, he beat all of us again. He laughed at the fact that Betty's teacher had been foolish enough to hit him, a poor, crippled man. My father not only knocked the teacher down the stairs; He had gotten him fired for striking a parent. The school never pursued child abuse charges and my father was once again free to continue his reign of terror.

Now! There was nothing stopping him and we were convinced there was no way out for us. Everyone that had tried to help had been either beaten up or had died. There was nobody that could help us. Our neighbors, teachers, doctors and clergy had all failed. Despite a lack of bars, we were locked in a prison, animals closed off from the world about us.

Still, even this didn't seem to please him. My father's need for control became an addictive habit. He craved even greater power over us. Not satisfied with the control over our emotional and physical well being, he now wanted to control our very minds. Perhaps he figured out that one could block things from their mind, like the time he allowed Jerry to rape me. This I had done, leaving the shell I resided in to endure the pain, while my mind was free to wander far from that pain, the humiliation and the suffering I was forced to endure. How could one look into the eyes of another living soul, knowing they too, were victims of our father's sick sexual perversions?

One night, my father awakened Betty and me. He said it was time. We were taken into the kitchen and ordered to sit on the floor. My father and his friends had already been drinking. I watched as my mother entered the room. She was bloody and appeared dazed, confused. They ordered her to sit on the kitchen chair; they had placed in the middle of the kitchen. They all wanted to be able to see. Mother begged him not to do anything stupid. I didn't know what was going to happen and just sat there watching as father pulled out a big pocket watch. He dangled it in front of my mother, swinging the watch back and forth, again and again. At first, I saw mother's eyes following the motion of the watch. Then her eyes went vacant, devoid of life; they showed no emotion at all. Her very soul placed into a container, stored for use whenever my father chose to snap his fingers.

I watched horrified as my father ordered my mother to crawl about the floor barking like a dog, in front of his friends and some strangers. Then she was forced to have sex with every man present, including the strangers. As my mother dressed, one of the men slipped something to my father. I didn't see what it was because he slipped it into his pocket quickly. My mother had returned to her chair as if awaiting more orders. For no apparent reason my father snapped his fingers. Then, I saw in my mother's eyes, the fear and the confusion. She had no idea of what had happened to her. Everything seemed as it had been before, the strange men were gone and the hours had seemed like mere minutes. She had once more been victimized and she had no knowledge of it.

I wanted to hide under the table but my body was frozen with fear. I felt a terror in me, like I had never felt before. Why! Did Betty and I have to watch that? Why? What was he planning now? I willed my body to move. Each movement sent shivers of fear throughout me. Soon, I would no longer be a human being. He would control my body, my emotions and my mind. I would become a zombie, a sexual plaything for him and his friends

That night I lay in bed wanting to cry but there were no more tears, even my tears had betrayed me. I was alone. Betty too, was silent. She also had closed her eyes trying to shutoff the pain we would soon endure. Though no words were spoken between us that night, we each knew what the other was thinking. We were doomed!

The next night Betty and I were awakened by our father again. This time in the kitchen, there were three chairs, one for each of us. My father and his friends stood leering at us. There, in the kitchen my mother, sister and I were told to sit on the chairs. I swore that I would kill myself before the night was over. I would die with dignity… no one would control me… no…. one!!!

Snap! Suddenly I heard the door close. I looked around and everything was as it was before. My mother, Betty and I still sat on the chairs. At first, I wondered if anything had happened. Then the small-darkened room shone brightly as the lights of a car backed out of our driveway. As I slowly stood up, I refused to let my eyes meet those of my father's. I knew they would mirror intense satisfaction. I stared at the chairs we had sat on; there in Betty's and mine, was the evidence of our nightmare. It! Had happened!

With my head low and my body aching, I retreated to my safe haven. There I lay, curled into a ball, holding tightly to my sister. We never spoke of those nights. Every time we were summoned to the chairs, we were fed better the next day. In fact, we were even given permission to eat with the family. However, his addiction to sexual perversions soon craved something new. It wasn't long before my father realized that the hypnotism had a flaw. We did not remember! So one day he decided to show me just what happened during those hours of hypnotic trance. There I sat on the cold floor as several strange men entered the house. Betty was forced to sit on the chair and I watched in horror as she was forced to perform whatever sexual perversion the five men wanted. Afterwards, each man handed my father money.

There I sat terrified. He had used our bodies for money. We were his prostitutes. He turned to me and said sharply, "Vina! It's time for you to sit on the chair and earn your keep!" I begged him to stop but he only laughed and placed my malnourished body on the chair. Then he began swinging the watch.....back.....and ...........!

Father soon tired of hypnotism and once again his sick obsession took over, craving new heights of depravity. He purchased a big black dog, which he named Gentle Ben. I was terrified of the dog. He had never bitten anyone but I would not go near him. There I lay in my safe haven watching him, as he lay by the table waiting for me to crawl out but I never did.

One night I heard the dog growling furiously. My father had him by the throat, dragging him. I had slowly crawled onto the living room floor, when I saw my father slap the dog. Bite Him! I begged, Bite, him Hard! I lay there quietly and I saw my mother. She was crying. Then I heard her scream, begging on her knees. I didn't know what was going to happen to her, so I crawled closer to the kitchen. My father's friends were in the laundry room. I saw one of them grab my mother and they pushed her down onto the floor between the kitchen and the laundry room. Her screams pierced my ears. As two of the men held her down, my father continued to fight with the dog. Oh God! What were they going to do to her? The moments that followed filled me with revulsion. Although the dog fought furiously, my father had his way as usual. There on that cold floor, held by my father's friends, my mother was forced to have sex with the dog. Screaming and begging them to stop, she fought them with all her strength but it was to no avail.

I was sick, unable to watch any more. I had to run, go to my safe haven. Shaking with fear, I ran without thinking. I had almost made it to the table when I felt my father's arm about me. "You are always in the way! I should have killed you years ago, but I didn't! I have spent the last nine years feeding and taking care of you and all you have given me is misery!" I felt his hand around my throat and I prayed he would kill me quickly. As he lowered my body down to that cold floor, my mind wandered, images of the rocking chair, and the smell of tobacco on my grandfather's sweater, the white painted house and the promise swirled through my mind.

I awoke in my safe haven, on the cold kitchen floor. My body lay there, aching, bruised and bloody. The dog, Gentle Ben, lay beside the kitchen table. His body stiffening, as his life faded from those glazed eyes. Had he tried to protect me and paid the price others had? I petted my dog and cried.

That Sunday I went to church. I sat in Sunday school wondering what had happened the night before? Had my father subjected me to my mother's ordeal or had the dog turned on father and been beaten to death? Perhaps, my grandfather had arrived before anything could happen. I know I would not be alive if not for the intervention of my grandfather. Busy trying to sort out my thoughts, I hadn't realized that the Sunday school teacher had sat down beside me. "Vina! Are you okay," he asked? I turned to him and quickly answered, "No!" He continued talking, "If you need anything, you can come to me. I've noticed your brother eating cigarette butts from the ashtrays. Do you have enough food at your house?" Without thinking I asked, "What happens when God gives a person to much to handle?" He knelt down beside and whispered, "If God gives you more than you can handle, he'll send an angel down to help you. Vina, what's wrong?"

I went to the altar and knelt down before the cross. There I prayed, "God, please help my family, for we have not sinned. Please end the beatings, the sexual assaults and the starvation forced upon us." Taking Chiefy by his hand, we slowly walked out of the church.

As I opened the door, I felt the wind blow across my face. I pulled my long hair back and smelled the aroma around me. Tobacco, I knew that odor well.

# 5. Rebellion

August 22, 1969 my father was drunk once again. He was angry at the whole world. As we watched him screaming and beating our mother, we knew that it would soon be our turn. The usual line up from hell, with him beating the eldest first, and then working down the line to the youngest. The terrible beatings would continue until we were unable to sit much less stand. This night, would bring a change, father seemed different. The beatings didn't satisfy him. Chiefy the youngest, now four years old wandered into the living room. Although father had yelled at him before about it, there he was eating a cigarette butt. It was something he just enjoyed doing.

We watched in horror, as father with his eyes ablaze with anger grabbed him. Father in a rage, shook him severely for several minutes, and then suddenly stopped. Chiefy was ordered to stand still. My father took out a cigarette and lit it up. After taking one puff, he pulled Chiefy closer and without warning slowly inched the cigarette towards his eye. Our father showed no remorse as he pushed the cigarette into his eye. Chiefy's screams filled the house, asking mother to help him but as usual she just stood with that vacant stare on her face. We all wanted to help him but our minds were terrified and our bodies frozen in fear. Chiefy was probably blind!

That was the last straw, it was either turn in our father or forget any chance of our survival. We had to declare war. Bob the second eldest, knew our only way to survive depended on him. Bob was allowed to leave the fenced in black top for short periods of time. About 7:00pm that evening, he left the house and ran over to a neighbor. There he asked to be taken to the police station so he could report the abusive situations that existed in the household. He told the neighbor that the abuse had become too intolerable and he could not watch the daily abuse of his family any longer.

After awhile my father began to wonder where Bob was. As the time grew later he began to question us. He became angry. This wasn't like Bob and he wanted answers. Our father had to be in control and now he was not and his anger mounted. Bob had not obeyed and he would be punished. Until he returned, each of us would pay. We were told to come into the living room, but none of us knew where Bob had gone. We had an unspoken pact that none of us would betray the others. It was either all of us together or nothing; our lives now depended upon it.

Later that evening, several police cars arrived in front of the house. Our father yelled, "Bob has done it this time! He is being brought home in the back of a cop car. I hope they take all of you. You kids go into the bedroom and don't say a word!" Knowing something was wrong, we moved closer to the door to listen. We could hear our father talking to the officers, "What has my son done? If he needs money to stay out of jail, keep him, he's not worth it. My children are bad and I have punished them often, especially Bob who will say and do most anything to get attention. I have tried to be a good father but their mother has had an evil influence on them."

By this time, we could hear my mother screaming and throwing herself about the room. This was not that unusual for her to do. In a small house, one can hear everything and when she was mad, she always lost control. I wonder now, if she threw the temper tantrum because she was losing us or if she just wanted attention. Which ever it was, it didn't work. The police officers didn't care about anyone. They just wanted to wrap up their investigation and finish their reports.

After awhile one of the officers opened the bedroom door and asked us to come into the living room. They had us line up starting with the oldest. Were they going to beat us too? The officer asked us our names and ages. Down the line we replied, "Allen sixteen, Betty thirteen, James eleven, Vina nine, Tommy seven and Chiefy four." The officer wrote the information for his report just as I had seen it done a hundred times on television. We were being arrested. After all the information was taken, we were told to follow one of the officers. While walking to the cars, I heard my mother yell. I turned as she reached for her youngest screaming, "Don't take my baby! You can have all the rest of them. Just don't take my baby! Please give me my baby!"

As I walked to the cars with my brothers and sister, I felt like I was being arrested. The cops were taking us away. An officer was still talking to my parents in the house but somehow I felt that they were not being punished. *WE WERE!* After all, it was us that were being placed in the cop cars. My parents would remain in the house living happily ever after and we would be sentenced to prison for the rest of our lives. This was not what I had imagined about the house in the dream. It was suppose to disappear from my eyes, back away from me. I thought it was my escape, my salvation but instead it was another means of punishment. At least in the house, I could hide under the table with the mice. Now! There was nowhere to hide.

As I was leaving the house, I noticed it was not moving. But the vision had reappeared once again. Somehow, I knew that this was the sign. Call it a gut feeling but I just knew. Where was grandfather? Was I missing the sign? Maybe I should run? Would they shoot me? I watched Allen and Betty enter the back seat of the police car that Bob was waiting in. They were placed in back just like criminals. I looked into their eyes they were filled with fear. Then it was my turn as an officer led James, Tommy, Chiefy and me to an unmarked car. Chiefy was placed on the lap of an officer and the rest of us were placed in the back. We sat there quietly for what seemed forever but in actuality it probably lasted only ten or fifteen minutes. However, when your world is changing before your eyes, moments can be an eternity.

I remember Chiefy's cries; he was only four years old. His arms reached to us but the officer jerked him back. He began to scream. At first I was jealous. I flashed back to the moment in the house when my mother had only screamed for him, why not for the rest of us? Her words burned into my mind, "Please give me my baby! You can have the rest of them." Her screams continued to echo in my ears, just as they had then. I can still picture the smile on my father's face as the police lined us up. He knew that he was rid of us. He never tried to keep us. He was happy!

When the officers were both in the car, they never spoke to us. Neither tried to comfort us or explain what was happening. It seemed like we were not important. James sat there quietly, never uttering a word. Tommy on the other hand was trying desperately not to cry. The car began to roll and for some reason I got on my knees and I looked back at the house. It began to back away, slowly getting smaller and smaller until it disappeared. And when there was no sign of the house, from out of nowhere I heard my grandfather say, "Vina!

It is time to be strong, you are not alone, and I am with you, just as I promised I would be."

This was not a dream however. This was real. We had been forced to abandon our home and all our belongings, such as they were. We left with the clothes on our backs, the rags we had worn that day. All our possessions had been left behind. Although we had very little, we were never given a chance to take anything. The officers didn't know, perhaps we had a favorite toy or a teddy bear or something that would have brought us comfort. I cannot remember having anything that would have brought me comfort. My sister and I didn't even own a doll. My father said girls were lower than dirt and therefore not worth spending money on. But the police officers didn't know that, how could they? We were just another case, commonly referred to as a number in their files. Numbers are not human and therefore have no feelings. We were to be sentenced for crimes committed as bad kids and at that point in my life I wasn't sure what good or bad kids did. Our exposure to the world had been extremely limited.

We were taken to the juvenile home. While waiting in line for processing, Betty said between tears, "They put us in the back seat of the police car. There were bars between the seats and the windows and the doors were locked. The three of us were prisoners. We are being arrested. They believe we are bad kids because that is what father told them. He always told us that nobody would believe us. He said we were evil children and if anyone found that out we would be sent to jail. Well, where are we now? In a jail for evil kids! Our father was right; he won!"

At the juvenile detention center, bars covered the windows and what appeared to be uniformed guards patrolled the hallways. I stood there in line wondering if I would get a jail cell, just like they had on television? Our father had finally gotten his wish. He was rid of us. I knew he would never step foot into a jail cell but we had.

While standing there, I saw a woman police officer; walk over to Chiefy, who was holding onto my hand. The officer told him that he had to go with her. I told the officer that I would watch him but she glanced at me as if I was a criminal. She sharply replied, "I will take him to where someone shall love him. He still has a chance, unlike the rest of you." She turned and asked me how old he was and I said, "He is three." His arms reached out for me as she walked away with him. I listened to his screams as he was taken away and I lunged to grab him but another guard grabbed me. As he was led away I yelled out, "Chiefy! I promise I will find you. Even if it takes forever, I will find you!"

By this time, my older siblings were done being questioned by the officers and they asked where Chiefy was. I told them what had happened. Allen looked at me and then began to yell at whoever would listen, "Chiefy isn't three, he's four years old! Bring him back here!" But it was too late, Chiefy was gone and it was my fault. After that, we decided that we had to escape. Allen said he'd get one of the cars that we had hid from father in and he would drive us up north. It would be our only hope; if we stayed here we would never see each other again.

We were separated and placed into different rooms. We had been questioned and examined by numerous people by this time. We were not allowed to talk to the others. No one knew where the others were or what was happening to them. We were all exhausted and very scared. After the questioning, I remember walking down a long corridor filled with kids, some were crying and others screaming. I remember my sister waiting in the middle of a hall. She looked lost and afraid. I ran to her and we embraced, crying as we held on to each other. At least we were together! We were told that our brothers had been taken to the other side of the home.

Another one of the employees came over and we were told to follow her. She led us to a room in another hallway. It was the shower room and we were instructed that we must take a shower before we could be taken back to our room. There was a girl in the shower room, who had a worker slapping and scolding her. It was later discovered that her father had attempted to drown her and had molested the girl. The young girl was deathly afraid of water. Who was worse I wondered, the father or the protection officer? I froze, was I next to endure the same treatment the poor girl was receiving? It was Betty and I, who now were being yelled at by the worker, telling us to get in the shower and scrub ourselves thoroughly. She didn't want any diseases brought into her establishment. I remember saying to Betty, "We have to escape!" She replied, "We will but not tonight. It must be midnight and we have to find the boys."

When we finished with our showers, we were shown to our room. Betty and I were placed in the same room. Our part of the center was referred to as the free side. I was happy that Betty and I were together; I did not want to be left alone. We held each other tightly and we cried. As we looked around our room, we saw one small window. It was barred. Those black iron bars seemed to be everywhere that night in the police cars and there in our room. A room meant for bad people, we were so afraid, unsure what life had waiting for us.

There were no pictures on the walls or stuffed animals on the beds, only the two twin beds with very thin surplus blankets. There was nothing that would offer comfort to children that might not be used to staying at a strange place. We had always slept together and I felt that this night was not one in which I should start sleeping alone. We were both terrified and could not sleep, so we talked for hours. We felt that as long as we could hear the other, then we were safe. It was very late when I drifted off to sleep. We were both red eyed from our tears and tired from recurring nightmares that interrupted our sleep. The emotional stress caused me to wet the bed that night. When the guard entered our room, she immediately noticed the wet bedding. Betty claimed she had an accident during the night and the guard took her outside the room and spanked her. Betty never told them that I had done it, after all a big sister has to protect her younger one. I felt I deserved whatever punishment was meted out because I had let them take Chiefy. I deserved to die.

In the community room, we were reunited with our brothers, all but Chiefy that is. God! I missed him, we all did. None of us were use to being away from home. There was one television in the room and if everyone would agree on what to watch, then the television would be turned on and we could see a program during our scheduled time. We were never allowed to do anything unless it was a scheduled period including meals, swimming and the television in the community room.

The other half of the detention center was known as the lock-down side. The regulations were much worse at that side. My brother's rooms were over there. On special occasions they were allowed to visit with us in the community room. This was an infrequent happening and then it was closely supervised. The children on their side had all been convicted of committing a crime and my brothers wanted to get out of there as fast as they could. They promised they wouldn't leave without us girls.

No one ever visited us. We were alone. All we had were each other and we pledged to stay together, no matter what the future might unfold. Almost all the other children had visitors. We watched as their parents hugged and kissed them in greeting and farewell. We knew we would receive no visitors in this place. After all who wants to visit bad kids in a children's prison? We knew that by now our father had convinced everybody, what had happened was our fault.

We remained under lock and key, looking at those black wrought iron bars, like the criminals we thought we were. We were forced to do things, like scrubbing the floor with toothbrushes before going to bed. After a day or two we decided to escape. I think the boys could have made it but they wouldn't leave without their sisters. That night Betty and I were ready, we heard their whistle but so had the guards. As soon as we left our room, guards came running and captured us. I watched the guards take my brothers back to the lockdown side. I knew their punishment would be harsher than anything we were to receive; Betty and I were given a couple swats on our bottoms and made to clean the baseboards with the toothbrushes. We were not allowed to sleep that night. Each time we fell asleep we were awakened with a swat. I remember the guard saying, "If you were good kids, do you think you'd be in here? Your own father told us to keep all of you. You are both so bad even he doesn't want you. The judge will take care of you!"

The next day was worse. We had a stricter time schedule. We were not allowed out of the guard's sight and there seemed to be more of them about. They were always watching us, yes we were criminals and this was definitely our prison.

One morning at breakfast, I remember being angry at the world. I watched the other children with their visitors and parents. We had nobody but ourselves. We had been given a hard- boiled egg and a slice of toast that day so I tossed my egg at a guard. The egg hit him in the back of his head. When he turned to see who had thrown it, the entire room was throwing their eggs. It was my most memorable food fight.

Shortly after arriving there Betty had started her period. At home father had always given her a cloth diaper to wear. One of the female guards gave her a tampon to use. She had never used one before and did not know how or what to do. When she asked the worker for help, she was laughed at and told to figure it out herself. After Betty placed the tampon inside her, she began having flashbacks of our father raping her. The workers thought she was cramping and ignored her cries. I asked Betty if she said anything to the guards and she replied, "When I asked the lady for help, she looked at me like I was stupid. If you had never seen one before, how would you know how to use it?"

One hot summer day in August, the social workers took all the children from the home swimming. Unlike most pools, this one was shallow at both ends, with the center being the deepest section. Everyone had to go into the pool. I was just about to get into the water when I saw my sister was drowning. Fortunately, my brothers were already in the pool. I remember Bob, yelling for somebody to help her but everyone was laughing and his shouts for help went unheard. Even the guards didn't respond. Somehow Bob, who couldn't swim either, managed to rescue her. Betty would have drowned because the guards had made no attempt to help her.

One day Betty disappeared. I walked all over the home but she was nowhere to be found. I finally asked a worker if she had seen her. She stated that Betty had a toothache and had been taken to the dentist. I knew that she was lying to me. When Betty finally returned she told me that she had to talk to a judge and some other people. She wasn't sure what was going to happen to us but she had asked the judge to keep us girls together. The judge told her that he had talked to the workers in the home and they had agreed that we appeared very close and that he should not separate us.

At the home, nobody liked us, not the workers, the guards or even the other kids. We were different, we did not fit in even there and we sensed we were not welcomed. There were no social workers, psychiatrists or psychologists appointed to talk to us. Nobody attempted to explain what was happening to us. All we had been told was that our parents did not want us back! Therefore we would have to earn our keep. Scrubbing the floors and baseboards would instill respect in us for the workers who were our overseers. Although we had never done anything to offend the workers, they did not like us. We were evil, we didn't have any clothes, we asked to many questions. We were very burdensome to them. The other children teased us unmercifully, saying we would grow old in the prison and never get out. I certainly believed them.

I remember one afternoon when a couple of boys grabbed me and pulled me into the boy's bathroom. They forced my head into the toilet and said, "Your face is funny looking but maybe the pee water will make it look nicer, then your father will want you!" They ran from the bathroom when they heard someone approaching. As I turned, I saw a frowning male guard. He pulled me by the back of my hair and said, "What are you doing in here little girl? Are you trying to see a naked little boy? You are being very bad and I have to punish you." I was told to pull down my panties, terrified I flashed back to my father and his friends, was this happening again? Is that all I'm good for? Please God! No more! The Guard just swatted my bottom several times, hard enough so that I was uncomfortable sitting down for the rest of the day.

A couple days later, I began to sense that something was wrong. Red flashes appeared from nowhere. I knew something was going to happen. At nine years old I didn't know what premonitions meant, even if I had what would I have been able to do about them? I was summoned to a room to speak with one of the workers. She told me that Tommy and I had been so good lately that they decided to reward us by taking us to a nearby store and getting us ice cream cones. The red flashes became more intense; I knew that they were lying. I stood up and said, "I want to say good-by to my sister." That upset the worker, who began to yell at me. She said that we would only be gone a short time and then I would be brought back to my sister. I told her that we didn't want any old ice cream. We hadn't been good kids; in fact we had been in several fights just recently. But as usual, I was not given a choice and I didn't want her to take Tommy by himself. He was only seven and he needed a big sister.

Tommy was so excited; he wanted a chocolate ice cream cone. I told him we were not going to the ice cream store but he replied, "Yes we are. They told me I could have ice cream. This is the first time anyone ever told me I was a good boy. What kind are you getting, Vina, they told me the truth didn't they? I was a good boy, wasn't I? Why don't the others get ice cream?"

Tommy and I looked out the window as the car began to pull away. Something deep inside told me, that not only were we not getting ice cream but that we would not return to the home. We had just lost three brothers and our sister. The only family we now had left consisted of the two of us. We were all alone. Why was God punishing us? God! Why couldn't anyone believe that we were the victims? We were not bad people. Everything I loved was disappearing. I would cherish Tommy as long as I possibly could, even if that meant only minutes. He was the only family I had now. I had lost my sister and she had lost us. I had always been with her and now she was alone. I had never told her how much she had meant to me, that she had been my hero.

At this point, I was not even sure whether they would separate Tommy and me. I had just lost most of the people I loved. I swore if they separated us, I would kill myself. I would not live without him. I don't remember the rest of the drive; a black cloud obscured everything.

That was the last memory of my sister Betty. Many years would pass before I was re-united with the woman she had become. Sisters, who like the legendary Phoenix, had arisen from the ashes to be reborn.

# 6. Last Farewell

As we pulled up to a two-story home, our caseworker told us to be quiet and to smile. She wanted us to make a good impression. We just stood there not sure of what to do, as an older woman opened the door and motioned us into the house. My mind began to wander; it was unlike the caseworker to take us visiting. One thing was certain; we were not going to an ice cream store. Upon entering the house, the caseworker engaged the older lady in a quiet conversation. I had no idea what was happening. Then, I heard the older lady say that she had only been expecting one child. She wasn't sure if she had room for two children. I prayed, "Please God! Keep Tommy and me together." The worker explained that no other homes were available and that it would only be for a short time. Then she would remove one of us to another foster home.

The older lady agreed to keep both of us for a short period of time. The caseworker told her that the court would issue a clothing allowance check in a day or two. However, for the moment the clothes we had on and an extra change of clothing was all we had. She would have to make do with them until the check arrived. We had no worldly possessions, just what the state had provided for us.... We were homeless and destitute.

At Mrs. Smith's house, there was another foster child. I think she was a lot older than me, maybe sixteen years old. Mrs. Smith had allowed her to stay for a couple years because in her words, "She earned her keep." After Mrs. H, our caseworker left we were taken upstairs and shown our bedroom. It was a large bedroom with two twin beds. I had never been in a room this large. We took our belongings out of the paper bags and tossed them on a bed. We were told to go downstairs when we finished. That didn't take long so we went downstairs and sat on the couch. We didn't know what to expect, so we just sat there waiting. When Mrs. Smith came into the room and found us sitting on her sofa, she became very angry. She had many rules for living in her house and the most important one involved the couch. No children were allowed to sit on the couch ever! We were told that children were to sit only on the floor. We learned that rule fast. There was to be no running or jumping in the house at any time. All our clothes must be put away at all times. We were never to bother the other children she babysat for. When she was absent from the house, the older girl Laurie was in charge. If we disobeyed Laurie or broke any of the rules, we were to be sent back to the home.

Mrs. Smith told us that Laurie was supposed to help watch all the children. But at sixteen, Laurie was more interested in the opposite sex and Mrs. Smith was growing tired of fighting with her. She said the last thing she wanted was any more kids, so she wouldn't put up with any mistakes from us. She might consider keeping one of us but there was no way in the world she would keep us both.

Mrs. Smith then noticed that we didn't have appropriate school clothes. She said she would have to call the courthouse in the morning. Then, she went over the school rules. We were being ruled to death, I thought. After pausing a moment, she asked us how old we were? My mind went blank. I knew I had attended school before but could not remember the school, which grade I had been in or how old I was. Everything had gone blank I had lost my memory. The only things I could recall were the names and ages of my brothers and sister. I looked at Tommy and he too was having the same problem. We had blacked everything out. Our memories were gone. All we had in this world was each other. Mrs. Smith thought we were being foolish and began yelling. We had really made a good impression, everything had gone wrong.

She finally sent us downstairs, telling us to go play with the other kids. We watched them, they were happy, just being plain kids. Somehow I knew I was different, that I didn't belong. So Tommy and I just sat there never saying a word. When Mrs. Smith came downstairs and saw us sitting there, she exclaimed, "Why aren't you two playing?" We sat at the foot of the steps for nearly two hours when she yelled that dinner was ready. Again we unknowingly broke a rule. At the table Mrs. Smith informed us that, "You are only allowed to drink your milk after you had eaten your food. Otherwise you will fill up on the milk and not eat. Then the food will get wasted and I hate wasting food." Both our glasses stood empty. I had never eaten oriental food before so I just poked at it. I don't think it would have mattered what she made because I was not hungry. I had spilled my milk and now wasted the food. I was really fitting into Mrs. Smith's house, I thought to myself.

The next day she called the courthouse and after a lengthy talk with Mrs. H, she decided to enroll us in a local school. A couple days later, Mrs. Smith took Tommy and I shopping for school clothes. I was excited, although we couldn't purchase many outfits; I had never had a new anything. I had always worn the old hand-me-downs of Betty's or those that some other relative had cast off. I remember once that an aunt had brought over a shell top. My father thinking it was a dress sent me to school dressed that way. The other kids made fun of me for being so poor and not having any good clothes. I was so embarrassed. The teacher sent me home for lack of proper clothing.

During our shopping trip, I picked out three new dresses and the prettiest pair of shoes. I couldn't wait to try them on. I thought if I had a pretty pair of shoes, everyone would overlook the fact that my feet turned in so badly. Maybe then I wouldn't be made fun of. Mrs. Smith however, noticed how I walked and then made a couple phone calls. The next day she took me to a doctor and after I was examined he instructed her to take me to a different shoe store. She purchased the most ugly shoes I ever saw and I told her I wanted to wear the pretty ones. She then explained that the doctor had stated my feet needed to be corrected and that I wasn't to wear the pretty shoes.

It wasn't long after I had adjusted to living at Mrs. Smith's, that I noticed she was having trouble with Laurie. One night they fought so badly that Mrs. Smith had Laurie removed from her home. This was my chance! I went straight to Mrs. Smith the next morning and asked her if I could take Laurie's position. I would watch the kids, clean the house and go to the local corner store in exchange for keeping Tommy and me. She told me she would have to think about it.

During the months of September through February I cleaned her house daily. I watched the kids when she was babysitting. I washed the dishes and yes I even went to the local store to purchase a few supplies. She always gave me a list and the exact amount of money. One day I went to the store and purchased a gallon of milk, a loaf of bread and a pound of butter. Shortly after leaving the store, I tripped over my feet; the milk tumbled to the ground and smashed, spilling all over the sidewalk. I sat down and cried. I knew I would be sent away from Tommy, back to that prison for the bad kids. Mrs. Smith didn't like to waste food. A strange car pulled up to the curb and a tall man got out and asked why I was crying. When I explained what had happened, he took me back to the store and replaced the milk I had broken. He drove me to Mrs. Smith's house, I never knew his name but I thanked him several times before I got out of the car.

I started fourth grade while I lived at Mrs. Smith's. Tommy was in second grade. We seemed much older than our ages of nine and seven. We watched the other children laugh and play, seemingly without a care in the world. Everyday, when we went home, we didn't know if we would stay there or be sent back to juvenile detention. We might even be separated. Yes, we were different, we had no friends, or family and we could not take anything for granted. The other kids laughed and made fun of us, especially because of the way I walked and my ugly shoes. We were referred to as wards of the state and that meant nobody wanted us. I could endure all that, as long as Tommy and I were together.

Over the next couple of months, Mrs. H had to take me to the courthouse every week. I was left in a hallway to wait. When it was my turn, Mrs. H escorted me into the judge's chambers. I remember being very scared. My entire life had been turned upside down and this was the man that could decide where I was to live, with whom I was to live and anything else he wanted to decide.

After a few minutes, a man dressed in a black robe entered into the room. Two other men followed him. They just stood there staring at me. I froze. What are they going to do to me? I ran as fast as I could to the big wooden desk, crying loudly, I crawled beneath it. Every time they approached the desk I screamed as loud as I could. I would not let anyone near me, especially those men.

Finally, the judge got down on his hands and knees and tried to coach me out from under the desk. There was no way I'd leave the safe haven I wasn't going to move. He stood up and addressed the other men, "It's no use. She is terrified of us. I want to know why this little girl is afraid of men. Get a woman in here, Right Now!" After several moments a woman entered the room and sat down in a chair by a wall. She made no attempt to approach the desk but did start to softly speak to me. At first, she asked me my name and how old I was, until I eventually crawled from beneath the desk to sit beside her. Ten, maybe fifteen minutes later, the judge returned to the room. Keeping his voice level and keeping his distance from me, he asked, "Should I schedule her for a medical exam?" The woman merely nodded her head yes.

It was a day, maybe two later, when I was taken to the doctor's office. Mrs. H said the doctor wanted to examine me for school. The doctor told me to take off all my clothes and lay down on the table. I was petrified; did the doctor want to rape me? Was my father right? I had only been to a doctor a few times and I had never had to take my clothes off before. He told me to spread my legs and I did. He pushed a small metal instrument inside me, it was cold and I tensed up as it entered me. The doctor talked to me the entire time he was examining me. His reassuring voice relaxed me. Upon finishing his examination of me, he walked over to the table and with tear filled eyes said, "I'm sorry for what you have suffered. I will make sure that the judge never lets anyone hurt you again."

The next week, I had to talk to the judge again. This time he had a lady present. While I sat next to her, he stayed on his side of the room, never coming near me. He only asked me if I wanted to go home to my family. I told him, "No! I could never go home." He then asked what I thought he should do with me and I replied, "Kill me, I have tried and I failed. If you send me home, my father will kill me. I don't want him to have the satisfaction. Let me die with dignity!"

That was the last time I saw the judge. The outcome of the trial and his decision would directly impact my life. The actions and fears I displayed in his chambers and the findings from the medical examination easily enabled him to reach a decision. The physical and emotional stress was so overwhelming that I was spared from testifying in open court against my parents. I was protected from the drama of the trial and was reassured that I'd never be sent home.

It wasn't long before the holidays approached. Mrs. Smith gave us our first Christmas. She even had a tree. It was a huge tree, bigger than I had ever imagined. The sparkling lights cast a warm glow upon the room, creating a very festive atmosphere. We were not allowed to go near the tree and all the gifts that were beneath it. She had spent a lot of money on Christmas. Tommy and I wondered if

Santa Claus would come. Nobody had said that we had been bad, maybe this year he would bring us a gift.

As Christmas approached, both Tommy and I grew excited. This was something other kids had told us about but we had never experienced for ourselves. Once when we had visited our grandmother at her toy store, we had been allowed to pick out one toy for the family. Betty and I had looked at the dolls; she had many to choose from. After a few minutes, Betty and I decided on a doll from the top shelf. The boys were looking elsewhere and decided they wanted a football. It was easy for grandma to decide which toy to give us. The boys played football for hours and sometimes Betty was allowed to play. My feet being so bad, I couldn't run so I sat on the sidelines with Chiefy, who was too young to play. Betty and I never did get any dolls. If Tommy and I had a gift under this Christmas tree, it would be very special.

I remember grandma's house. She did not want to eat in the same house she went to the bathroom in. Eventually the state forced her to install the necessary sanitary requirements in her home. The last time we had visited her, that outhouse was still standing and functional. I enjoyed picking on my brothers and they always seemed to get even with me for doing so. One day while playing, hide and seek at grandma's house, one of my brothers told me to hide in the outhouse. He told me nobody would look in there. I didn't realize that it was a trick until they started rocking the outhouse back and forth. They wouldn't let me out and I started screaming. When my father came out to see what the yelling was about, my brothers stopped and ran off. They forgot to set the outhouse upright and over it fell, splashing me with the contents. I was drenched in sewage. This earned me another beating by my father and after that I no longer played tricks on my brothers.

The thoughts of Betty and my brothers caused me heartache. Christmas was almost upon us and I wondered what they were doing? Christmas is spent with families. Why couldn't Tommy and I spend ours with them? Would they even remember me? So much of my previous life was disappearing. Memories, like chalk erased from a blackboard. Vina had been removed from her existence, leaving only an empty shell. What would she become, once everything had been stripped away? I had no way of knowing.

I wondered why I couldn't remember? Occasionally, I would catch a glimpse of the past, only to watch it fade away. It was like watching television while slowly switching the channels. I would see their faces but I couldn't make out whom they were. What was wrong with me? Have I gone crazy?

The flashing lights on the tree brought me back to the present. Here I am sitting in front of a Christmas tree that stretches to the ceiling. Christmas is a happy time but suddenly I felt so very sad. Tommy glanced my way and said, "You look like you've seen a ghost, Vina." I turned and answered, "Only a ghost from my past, Tommy." He replied softly, not wanting Mrs. Smith to hear him, "I'm doing the same thing. One minute I'm here and the next I am back home. Vina, I'm afraid, it's like I'm being haunted by the past."

Mrs. Smith entered the room and saw us looking at the gifts under the tree. She sent us to our room after telling us the following, "Those are gifts for my family and I don't want you two tearing the wrapping paper. The court will decide if you are to receive a Christmas this year. I just barely had enough to buy my family's gifts. You children will just have to do without." I felt like a knife had been thrust deep into my heart. We had been good! I had cleaned her house, watched the bratty kids and ran errands as necessary. I had made the deal to earn my keep, which enabled Tommy and I to stay together and a deal was a deal. That was more important than celebrating Christmas with a gift. I was ten years old and I was grown up. Tommy wanted a GI JOE doll so badly, if only I could have bought him one but I had no money and I wasn't going to try stealing one. That was out of the question. I had already been in jail and wasn't going back.

The thought of stealing brought back another memory. Back home, how long ago that now seemed. I had gone to the store with James and my father. Being two years older than me, he would always pick on me and make fun of me. I think he just enjoyed making me mad. I use to hate that, now I missed him. While at the store this time, he stole a candy bar and hid it in my pocket, without me noticing he had done so. After leaving the store, my father noticed it and as always became very angry with me. "For stealing, you will not eat for a week! I'll make sure you never steal again! We are not poor people," he screamed at me.

Then after slapping me several times, I had to go into the store and confess to stealing the candy bar. Afterwards he ate the candy bar in front of me. My brother James just laughed at me but when we arrived home, he became mad and began to hit me saying it had been his candy bar. I yelled that I would hate him for the rest of his life. I never told him that he was forgiven. I knew that he stole the candy because; just like all of us he was hungry. He probably thinks I still hate him. Some day I'll find a way to tell him I forgave him.

"Why do you look like that Vina," Tommy whispered in my ear? "We never had a Christmas before, so don't be sad," he continued as tears formed in his eyes. I could do without Christmas being all grown up as I was but Tommy was only seven and he deserved a Christmas. I knew that Mrs. Smith wasn't religious but that night I prayed that God would forgive our sins and let Santa Claus bring Tommy one gift. I wasn't going to become greedy; I asked nothing for myself just that something be done for my brother. If God could forgive us maybe Tommy would get a big gift and would stop crying himself to sleep each night.

I tried to comfort him. Each night we would say our prayers and then while lying in our beds, we would recite the names and ages of our brothers and sister. I thought that should we become separated that he might be able to remember me. I wanted to be remembered. I loved him so much. He was all I had and I felt I couldn't go on without him. Although I never admitted it, I needed him as much as he needed me.

Every night we went to bed and fought sleep. With sleep came the fear that upon waking, one of us would be gone. Sleep was an enemy. To help us fall asleep, I would read to him. Every night over the past months, I read him the story of the Ten Little Indians. Now, I wonder if I read that story to keep in touch with the spirits. I had not felt grandfather's spirit in some time but I clung to the thought that he was near. Without that hope, I could not have carried on and Tommy never complained about the story, in fact he always fell asleep before I finished.

Just a day or two before Christmas, Mrs. Smith told me about the court trial. She stated my parents had lost custody of all their children and that I would never have to go home. It was now up to the courts to decide the fate of us children. Our stay at her house would soon be ending. The court had decided she was too old and they wanted us placed with a younger family. She was not sure if Tommy and I would be placed together but she had explained to the judge about how close we were. I promised her, that I would clean better; perhaps I could drop out of school and work all day. I would do anything if she would let us stay with her. Living at her house wasn't so bad, as long as one stayed off her sofa.

The thought of leaving her home increased our level of stress. The sleepless nights became more frequent. Each night I stared at the ceiling, wondering what life would have been like had I had parents who loved me? Then there were the moments I worried over Tommy. I wanted to take care of him, feeling like his mother, I was afraid of deserting him. My anxiety started showing in my school performance, my grades suffered. I became irritated with the kids at school. I became jealous of the fact that they did not have to work for a living. They had parents, who loved them. They didn't worry about where their next meal was coming from. They did not walk in fear of their father finding and killing them. The same God that had brought them peace on earth had deserted me. They might be my same age but emotionally I was so much older…so very much older!

Christmas had arrived. The house was filled with the aroma of pies and homemade bread baking in the oven. There were joyous sounds of laughter echoing throughout the halls, as the family members shouted Christmas greetings to each other. It was the season to be jolly and the people there were indeed that. Old Saint Nick had come the night before and left presents for the good girls and boys. Somehow when he made his list and checked it twice, Tommy and I were forgotten. There weren't even crumbs, from the cookies we had left by the door. We knew he had been here and had not left us anything. We just didn't deserve Christmas.

We sat on the ends of our beds crying, feeling sorry for ourselves. Everyday since Thanksgiving, I had prayed that God would grant Tommy a Christmas. For us, this day held nothing but sorrow. The louder the laughter from the festivities downstairs, the harder we cried. It shouldn't have mattered that much to us, we had never celebrated Christmas but just once we wanted to share in what other children had. Was that asking too much?

We were to busy crying to notice when Mrs. Smith entered the room. She stood there with the empty cookie platter and said, "Why don't you come downstairs? My family is here and I would like you to meet them. They've come a long way to celebrate the holidays with me." We wiped the tears from our eyes and went downstairs to meet Her Family, the People that had all the presents under the tree! We put smiles on our faces not wanting to spoil Mrs. Smith's holiday.

We watched as everybody opened the gifts until only two small packages remained under the tree, waiting to be opened. The gifts had no names written on them, just Merry Christmas from Santa Claus. Santa had come to the Smith's and left us out. Back home father would not have allowed him in the house, even had he tried to enter. Now he could come and go as he pleased and he had forgotten us. He hadn't cared.

As we slid back to the wall, I noticed the people were looking at us. We had interfered with their celebration. We stood up seeking to escape to our bedroom, where we could cry; pray, even shout out our frustrations. We would not let these strangers see us crying. It wasn't their fault that they had a family. They were not wards of the state! They belonged to society. They had homes and relatives to share the festive holiday with.

As we turned to leave the room, one of Mrs. Smith's family members stopped us and said, "Santa did not forget you two this year! We all wrote him a letter. The gifts under the tree were left for both of you." I tripped running to the tree, so Tommy beat me to the gifts. His face was beaming with joy, his eyes brighter than the lights on the tree. No words could ever describe the feelings we experienced at that moment.

We sat there on her sofa, yes even on the forbidden sofa, as the family watched us open our very first ever Christmas presents. I opened my gift slowly, being careful not to tear the pretty wrapping paper. Tommy meanwhile, tore off the paper as fast as he possibly could. Nope, Santa didn't bring a GI Joe. I think I should have been more detailed in my prayers but God was supposed to know everything, wasn't he? Tommy was just a little upset that he had gotten a truck, a toy that Mrs. Smith thought was more appropriate for a boy. GI JOE was a doll and only little girls played with dolls.

I was so happy watching Tommy, that I hadn't finished opening my gift. My first Christmas and I received two gifts. My prayers had been answered giving Tommy a Christmas and the one I opened. It was a color camera and I knew who I wanted a picture of more than anyone in the world, TOMMY and I wanted a picture of the two of us together. A picture for both of us, should tomorrow our lives be torn apart.

A few days later, a lady from the court stopped by she told Mrs. Smith that our normal caseworker was on holiday vacation, so she had been assigned to check on us. She was a loud voiced woman and we could hear her from the other room. I sat very still, not wanting her to know that I was listening. "The courts did not have enough money this year for the children's Christmas. There were too many homeless children and this was not a good year for us financially. These kids understand. I was told they never celebrated a Christmas anyway. Besides they are only wards of the state." Mrs. Smith became very angry and said, "These children have feelings. Did anyone consider that? They are human, just like the kids in other homes. My family and I chipped in enough money and bought them each a gift." The woman laughed and said, "Don't get to attached to them, the courts are still working on finding homes for these two. What did you get them?"

Mrs. Smith told the caseworker what each of us had received and I knew the woman sitting in the kitchen would want them. Mrs. Smith continued, "I don't really see what harm it did to get them something." When the woman stood up, she began speaking very softly and I had to creep closer to hear what was being said. My instinct screamed, "Don't trust this woman!" As their conversation continued, Tommy came walking down the stairs. When the lady saw him, she ceased talking to Mrs. Smith and said, "Hello Tommy. I hear you and Vina received Christmas gifts. Let me see what you got." Slowly we showed her our presents. The woman asked, "Vina, who are you going to take a picture of?" I proudly replied, "Tommy and I. One for each of us." I watched the lady's eyes as she said, "Let me take the picture for you." She did not speak the truth. Her eyes just as my mother had said so long ago, told a different story.

The picture I would cherish for the rest of my life. There stood Tommy and I both smiling happily. It was our picture, our keepsake, something to cherish if God forbid, we became separated tomorrow. Somehow I would remember and I hoped that the picture would keep my memory alive in Tommy. After the woman took the picture, she removed the film from the camera. "I will get these developed for you. Do you have anymore film?" she asked. "No," I answered, "Mrs. Smith will take the film to the store. Won't you Mrs. Smith? I want Mrs. Smith to do it!" I knew that I would never get my picture back. Whenever I glanced at the film in her hand, I saw the red flashes. Just like the previous warning I had received, I was being told something was happening that wasn't right.

The woman took the film when she left and with her the photographic memory of a brother I would cherish. Why did she want it, we meant nothing to her? Now, she was gone and so was my film. Mrs. Smith apologized saying there was nothing she could do. I cried for more film but Mrs. Smith replied, "The camera was a bad choice on my part. You can keep the camera but I'm not allowed to give you any more film. I'm sorry you can't have your picture."

January $10^{th}$ arrived, just a day like most others. I sat downstairs watching the children play in Mrs. Smith's basement but I was still not willing to play with these kids. They were normal children and I couldn't identify with them. The kids, Mrs. Smith babysat, belonged to loving families and they would go home with parents that hugged and kissed them. I could smell the aroma of baking coming from upstairs and Mrs. Smith was happily humming a tune. I hated the moment when the kids were picked up to go home. I could tell that their parents had missed them. They loved their children and that was something I would never know. Mrs. Smith treated me nicely but she didn't love me.

After the kids had gone home, Tommy and I went upstairs. There in the kitchen stood Mrs. Smith, with a chocolate cake in her hands. "Happy birthday to you! Happy birthday to you," sang Mrs. Smith as Tommy and I looked around the room to see whom Mrs. Smith was singing to. Nobody was there but us. "Vina, Happy birthday," a smiling Mrs. Smith said. Then she continued to explain, "Today you are ten years old and I baked you a birthday cake. You have to make a wish and then blow out all the candles. If you do that, you will have your wish come true." This would be an easy wish to make. I wished that Tommy and I would remain together living as brother and sister forever. I closed my eyes, made the wish and said a prayer that all the candles go out. Just before I started to blow, Tommy yelled, "Vina! Don't spit on the cake. I never have had cake before." I closed my eyes and blew as hard as I could. When I opened my eyes, all the candles were out, I had done it. My wish would now come true.

The weeks flew by, it was now the thirteenth of February and I continued our bedtime ritual, the reading of Ten Little Indians, which I could read from memory by now. I was tired and having difficulty reading. Tommy wasn't asleep yet and demanded that I keep reading. Finally we both fell asleep. I awoke to find a strange presence in my room. At the foot of my bed stood the image of a man, which seemed to glow in the darkness. For some reason I was not afraid of this person. I looked into his eyes as he stood there watching me. They twinkled with tenderness, telling me that their owner meant no harm to me.

Within seconds, he began to speak, "Tomorrow you will have to leave and I shall watch over Tommy. You must believe in me and in time I shall bring you both together again." The man then disappeared before my eyes. I remembered the conversation with the pastor at the church. God does not give you more than you can handle, well this time he did. I was devastated, I cried until the tears refused to fall. I lay there all night wondering what to tell Tommy in the morning? How could I tell him that I saw spirits or ghosts at times? Was that God last night? Was it my grandfather again? Am I crazy? Why is this happening to me?

Was my grandfather's spirit somehow guarding me through this difficult time? Perhaps, it was the spirits who were destroying my life. There are bad spirits aren't there? Everyone and everything I had known had left me or had been taken from me. I was alone and this time there would be no Tommy. Yes! I will be truly alone.

I packed my things after Tommy went downstairs for breakfast. I didn't have an appetite and it took just a brief time to pack the three outfits I owned. The courts had not sent any other money after the original check they had authorized for school clothes, when we were first placed with Mrs. Smith. I packed and repacked my clothes, preparing myself for what was about to transpire. I mustn't cry I must be strong for Tommy. Placing the Ten Little Indians upon his pillow, I knelt by his bed and softly whispered, "I leave this room with the promise that you'll take care of Tommy. Please give him the strength to carry on. Please keep my memory alive in his heart. I want him to remember the sister who loves him dearly."

As I silently cried my prayer, I felt a presence in the room with me. I felt a hand, come to rest upon my shoulder and without a spoken word; I knew Tommy would be safe. I turned to see who or what had touched me, but upon looking, I found nobody, just a cool breeze, which sent chills through me. But there upon the pillow, glowed the book, Ten Little Indians. Tommy would be watched over.

Mrs. Smith came into the room to check on why I had not come down for breakfast. She saw my packed belongings sitting on the floor. I looked into her eyes and asked, "Why didn't you tell me I was leaving?" She looked startled and replied, "Vina, I just received the phone call ten minutes ago. How could you have known that you were being sent to a new home? I was going to tell you after breakfast." With a sad smile, I responded with, "A friendly spirit told me."

I went downstairs but I couldn't look at Tommy. With tear-reddened eyes, I looked out the window to see snowflakes falling outside. We could have built a snow fort, I thought, or even a snowball fight. Instead I would be leaving my brother behind. The only remaining family I had left in this world and I would be deserting him.

Mrs. H arrived about an hour later. I stood at the door waiting. Tommy did not understand what was going on. He turned to me and said, "Vina, where are you going?" I opened my mouth to answer but no words came forth. The sounds had deserted me, just as I was about to desert Tommy. Mrs. H answered for me, "Tommy, she is going to get her haircut cut. Look how long her hair is. Don't you think your sister will look pretty with short hair?" "No!" he yelled, "I like her hair. Please don't cut it. Vina! What's wrong today? You haven't spoken to me all morning." There was nothing I could do to make our parting any easier. With my heart in my throat and without a further glance, I turned my back on my younger brother and walked away. Please forgive me little brother.

Mrs. H quickly drove away but that did not shut out the forlorn screams coming from Tommy's mouth. I should have said good-bye, I love you Tommy but I hadn't. I twisted in my seat and attempted to open the car door. I must tell Tommy good-bye, there was no shame in saying farewell to your loved ones. I was halfway out of the door when I felt Mrs. H grab me by my neck and pull me back into the vehicle. Mrs. H filled the car with profanities as she struggled to keep me within the moving automobile. The last words, I remember her uttering are, "You are an evil child, and you have the devil himself in you."

After she had gotten the car stopped, I was pulled from the car and slapped several times. She went to the back of the car and removed a piece rope from the trunk. Was she too, going to hang me? She quickly tied my hands and legs together so I could not escape. Then placed me back into the car and drove off in silence. This happened on Valentine's Day 1970, a day of love. Boy, did I ever feel loved. I vowed on that day that I would find Tommy, just as I had promised Chiefy, that I would find him. My young life was filling with oaths and vows, challenges to be overcome. I would spend my life searching for the family I had lost, neither the courts or Mrs. H would be allowed to interfere in that quest. I promise Tommy, I will find you! Somehow! Somewhere! Sometime! Good-bye……

# 7. Alpha & Omega

As Mrs. H drove away, I studied every street sign we passed. I was sure I could find my way back to Mrs. Smith's house and to my brother. Surely it wouldn't be that hard to do; after all we had only made a couple turns. In my mind, I mapped out all the streets we had used. I would escape tonight. There was a city park with benches near the entrance. I could sleep under the stars; I would not even be missed because I was nobody's child.

When the car stopped, we were right in front of the courthouse. Mrs. H took me inside and we walked down that long hallway that led to the judge's chamber. I paused at the door to the judge's chambers. Was it just a few short months ago, that I had spoken with the judge? I had begged him at that time to place Tommy and I in the same home. My mother had always claimed that one lacked dignity, if they had to beg. I had lost my dignity and I had lost all the family I had, when this man had scattered my brothers and sister to the wind. I had felt no shame in begging to stay with Tommy.

The thought of my mother's words brought back the bad memories, the cruel beatings and sexual abuse, the days without food and the leering looks of my father's friends. I could see the looks upon the faces of my brothers and sister, their eyes following me as I walked out of their lives. In my mind I had deserted them, I should have found a way to stay with them but I had not. With a stroke of a pen, the judge in his decision erased ten years of a family's existence.

"Vina," Mrs. H called my name, bringing me back to reality. "We have to stop off at my office for a few moments, while I make a phone call." After completing her phone call, Mrs. H turned to me and said, "I am taking you to a home for unwanted girls and there you shall spend the rest of your childhood. You will be required to earn your keep because it is not their responsibility to support you. You must obey and do what you are told, otherwise you will be sent back to the juvenile detention center. It is not the State of Michigan's fault that your parents did not want you. You have only yourself to blame for this mess."

When we left the courthouse, I am sure that Mrs. H deliberately drove in circles in an attempt to mislead and confuse me. She knew that I would try to escape and find my way back to Tommy, so she took no chances of that happening. I had actually pointed it out to her that she had gone down one street, twice already. She became very angry at this comment and she yelled, "You think that you are so smart, well your grades don't show it! There is absolutely no reason for your grades to be so low. It is hard enough with your looks, to find a family that is willing to take you into their home. With your poor grades, it has become damn near impossible. Just because you've lost your family, it doesn't excuse you from getting good grades in school. There was no justification for you failing fourth grade Vina!"

As we pulled into the driveway of the home, I noticed it was much to small to be a home for unwanted girls, unless of course there was only a couple of us. At least in this home I would fit in, after all we would all be unwanted girls, wouldn't we? Perhaps now I will find a friend. My nights would become much longer since Tommy would no longer be with me. My nightly ritual now had one more name and age to recite before I fell asleep. How could Mrs. H think that my school grades meant anything to me, compared to the destruction of my family and the loss of my brothers and sister? They meant nothing!

As we approached the house, a young woman opened the door and invited us inside. This isn't a shelter for unwanted children I thought. I think this is another foster home and they wanted another child. Mrs. H had lied to me again. I should have known not to believe her. What was the harm in telling me the truth? Didn't I at least deserve that? Am I going to grow up with nothing but lies for memories?

Over in a corner stood a boy who appeared to be a few years older than me. What was he doing there? Why couldn't Tommy have come? I heard Mrs. H talking, "She has trouble walking because of her disabled feet, which causes her to fall a lot. She has bad teeth, those will need attention and she has had a lot of emotional trouble in school. She doesn't exhibit a lot of intelligence, resulting in very poor grades at her last school. She does know how to perform housework so that is her only redeeming grace." My God! Did she think I was deaf too? I was standing right next to her as she said all that. Was I supposed to say, "Thank-you for calling me stupid, Mrs. H?"

There I stood watching the two women converse and I wondered what I should do, should I smile, take a seat on the sofa, what if she was like Mrs. Smith and sitting on her couch was forbidden too? Maybe she wouldn't like me and I could be sent back to Mrs. Smith and be with Tommy again. I'm scared, why doesn't somebody talk to me? Why have I lost my family?

The two ladies finally recognized my presence. I just couldn't listen to their criticisms and now they had caught me daydreaming. Oh well! They don't think I'm that bright anyhow. Mrs. H introduced me by saying, "Vina, this is Carol. She will be your new mother. Oh that reminds me. Carol! You must change her name. The judge stated in light of her testimony and her uncommon name, it would be in the best interests of the child to give her a new identity. It is a matter of her safety. The court is not sure what her father might do to her, if he ever locates her again. When that is done, just notify me."

A few minutes later Mrs. H had gone, leaving me alone with this strange woman, who was to become my mother? Carol looked at me and said, "I wonder just how stupid you really are? If you have a mental problem, I'll send you packing right back to where ever they found you. Let us get something straight between us, Missy! My husband Mark wants a little girl and in hopes of saving my marriage, I'll let you stay. You are not my child! I will give you a list of chores to be done everyday, see to it that they are done and in exchange I'll feed you. I will not tolerate a crybaby or a disobedient child. One mistake and you'll be gone. I don't want you!"

She then introduced me to Mike, her ten-year old son. Mike was an only child and as such was used to getting his own way. He quickly let it be known that he didn't want me living with him. Carol smiled smugly and told me, "Don't make yourself too comfortable because should Mark not like you, it obvious nobody else does either. The State cannot pay enough money for someone to take you in."

I was taken to my bedroom but told just to place my belongings upon the bed. She was sure that once Mark came home and saw what I looked like, I'd be on my way back to the home very quickly. So, I placed the brown paper bag containing my two changes of clothes on the bed. Those were my worldly possessions. I stood there at the foot of the bed fighting back my tears. I wanted to run but I knew I'd never find my way back to Tommy. After tomorrow, I too, would cease to exist. I had no family and tomorrow I would not have my own name. Nobody would ever be able to find me.

I heard Carol loudly call me. She had an irritating voice almost a bird like screech. I wiped the tears from my eyes and slowly walked down the hall, I remembered that she didn't like crybabies and I needed to regain my composure. I stood in front of my new mother, I really felt comfortable after that wonderful two-minute introduction Mrs. H had given. She had really extolled my virtues, hadn't she? "Veena! Or whatever you call yourself," she screeched, "Mark won't be home for a few hours yet, so you have time to get some chores done." I stood in the kitchen watching Carol make out a list of things that she wanted done. She thrust the list at me saying, "You can read can't you?" I quickly replied, "Yes." As I completed each task, I checked it off the list and then waited for Carol to inspect my work.

When, Mark arrived home, all the chores had been completed and met with Carol's approval. Now the hour of truth had arrived, I stood in the living room awaiting Mark's decision. My heart pounded as he bent down to look at me. Was I going to stay in this place? I prayed to be found unworthy and sent back to Mrs. Smith's but as usual my prayers went unanswered. Mark thought I was a very pretty little girl and would be a very nice daughter. So! I was to become Mark's daughter and his wife's bond servant.

Being it was Valentine's Day, Mark felt that we should celebrate and go out to a nice restaurant for dinner. Mark said that I could pick out the restaurant, yeah me, who had never been to one before. I really felt foolish so I turned to Carol and said, "Carol, you pick your favorite restaurant. That is where I would like to go." Carol smirked, saying, "Mark, maybe we should leave her home, after all she doesn't have any clothes that are appropriate for dinning out!" Mark just replied that I looked just fine and that he wasn't going without me.

We went to a nice restaurant, not far from where they lived. I thought it was very fancy but Mark assured me that my clothes were indeed appropriate and not to worry. Carol however, was of a different opinion; she felt I should be hidden in a corner so people wouldn't notice me. She had a social reputation that my presence seemed to tarnish.

Unfortunately for Carol, my table etiquette was severely lacking. After all, my parents hadn't cared if I ate or not, there was no training in the social graces at my house. It was obvious to me, that Carol had an image to uphold and that table manners were very important to this family. I tried to imitate Mark as best I could, but my utilization of knife and fork offended Carol, who complained the entire meal. At the end of the meal, Carol informed me that I had to place my fork on the table and chew each bite of food, thirty-two times. If she caught me cheating I would be removed from the table and not allowed to finish my meal.

Later that evening, when we had returned home, Mark and his wife discussed where I was to be enrolled in school. Carol wanted to wait a couple weeks because she felt sure that I was not going to fit into the family and that I would be going back to wherever Mrs. H had found me. Mark felt different, saying that I should be enrolled as soon as possible so that I wouldn't fall to far behind, especially if I was having difficulty with my studies. Mark told Carol, that she should take the next day off from work and buy me some new school clothes. She was also to take me to court and have my name changed legally. He said this shouldn't take more than a day.

Mark included me in the discussion as to what my new name would be. Carol did not care for any of the names I had picked out and decided that I should be called Kimberly. The next day we were in Mrs. H 's office at the courthouse. Would I ever escape from that place? We stood at Mrs. H's desk with the necessary paperwork to establish my new identity. In our discussions the night before the subject of a new middle name had never arose, so when it became an issue, I asked to be allowed to keep my middle name. Although Mrs. H didn't like it, she relented after I argued that I should be allowed to keep something that was mine. I had lost my home, my parents, my brothers and sister, and now my first and last names. I intended to keep something that was *me* even if this was to be a new beginning I wanted my middle name.

After becoming Kimberly, Carol took me shopping for school clothes and then enrolled me at Mike's school. Mike and I attended a parochial school but the increased costs brought about by my tuition meant that we had to walk home from school rather than ride the bus. We walked the two miles home each night. My first day at school was a disaster. The teacher asked a simple question, one that, any fourth grader should have been able to answer. What is your name? For the life of me, I could not remember my new name. The teacher thought I was playing the role of class clown and asked if anyone in the class knew whom I was. Of course nobody knew and even Mike sitting in the row next to me, denied having any knowledge of my name.

It didn't do any good in attempting to explain to my teacher, who not wanting to listen to my explanation sent me to the principal's office. Here too I was asked my name, this time by the principal but knowing my name had changed I still could not recall what Carol had named me. After several attempts accompanied by a swat on my bottom, my file was pulled and Carol received a phone call at her office. Carol arrived at the school extremely upset but I was only suspended for the duration of the day. As a punishment I was given a homework assignment, which entailed the writing of my name one hundred times. Carol never attempted to explain that my name had been changed the previous day; she only apologized for my behavior.

When we arrived home, Carol slapped me several times and told me I should be ashamed of myself for behaving as I had in school. Then she made out a list of chores that had to be completed before I was allowed to eat. I worked the rest of the day completing the tasks in each room. I was famished by the time dinner was ready but not having finished the list nor done my homework assignment, I was not allowed to eat. While the family ate dinner, I wrote my new name one hundred times.

It was bedtime when I finished my assignment. I was exhausted and I retreated to my new safe haven, shutting my bedroom door as I sought peace. I closed out my new family and I recited each name and age from my old family. Sleep eventually overtook me and I drifted off into a deep slumber, disturbed only by the nightmares that were to shadow my existence for years to come. In my dreams I saw the starvation, the beatings, the bruised bodies, the sexual assaults all the actions that tore my family asunder, I relived my past, over and over and over.

I was startled by the alarm clock, which awakened me for my second day of school. Although this day was uneventful compared to my first, I impatiently waited for the bell to sound, signaling the end of the day. As the hours dragged, I was subjected to whispered laughter from my classmates. Mike had told them, that I was so ugly; my parents had given me away. The other kids now made fun of me, as the bell rang I ran from the classroom, once again I was alienated. The one who did not belong!

Feeling sorry for myself and alone in the world, I left the schoolyard and ran down the street. I wasn't paying attention to my surroundings; I never thought I would get lost. I was suddenly walking along a road and I had no idea where I was and I didn't care. A convertible suddenly pulled alongside of me. The teenage guys in the car yelled for me to come over. I strolled over to the car listening to their laughter. As I approached the car one of the boys yelled, "Don't you know better than to come to a stranger's car? What kind of parents have you got? Don't they teach you anything?" I stood in front of the car and told the boys I didn't care and as a matter of fact no one in the entire world did.

"Are you lost," one of them asked. Turning and walking away I replied, "No!" Then to my surprise, I heard Mark's voice, frantically, yelling my name over and over. He jumped from his car and ran to me. For the first time in my life an adult cared. Mark picked up my tiny body and hugged me so tightly that he took my breath away and carried me to the car. With tears streaming down his cheeks, he explained that he had driven around for three hours searching for me. He said that Carol had even called the police, to report me missing.

When Mark and I arrived home, we discovered that Carol had not notified the police. She had been certain, that I was never in harms way. "Look at her, Mark. Who would want her?" was her retort, when asked by Mark, as to why she hadn't called the police. She then asked her husband to pick up some groceries at the store. While Mark was gone, I received a spanking with a wooden paddle because I had not completed my daily chores.

When Mark, returned home, he informed his son that he was to walk me home from school each night until I became better acquainted with the neighborhood. Mark was genuinely concerned that I might have been kidnapped or injured but he was the only family member that cared. I cannot describe how nice I felt, knowing that somebody cared what happened to me.

With Mike's help, I eventually learned the way home. The way he taught me was longer than the one he normally took. He was taking after his mother and he didn't want to be seen with me, it spoiled his reputation with his friends. After a few weeks, I knew my way well enough to walk it alone. Although it took a little longer, I was quite happy to be walking without Mike and his friends. On my way home, I walked past the public school. These children didn't make fun of me, I was considered normal. I had started walking with a couple girls, who were my own age. Suddenly! I had some friends.

There were a couple times that I walked too slowly and my tardiness caused me to fall behind in accomplishing my chores. This resulted in Carol spanking me with the paddle. In all likelihood she would have found another excuse to do so. The spankings were becoming a daily occurrence. So the extra time spent with my friends, was worth the beating I knew I would get. My relationship with Carol was steadily getting worse. It seemed the more that Mark liked me, the more she hated me.

It wasn't long before a girl named Cindy and I became the best of friends. We shared secrets but I never spoke of my past because of the deep shame it invoked. I knew what had happened to me was not normal behavior. Not every woman or girl was subjected to that kind of abuse. Mark had tried to be a good father and had never laid a hand on me. Through him, I learned I could trust some men, that I was a normal little girl and not a sex object.

The nightmares continued however, the past continued to haunt me. Just as before, the night remained my enemy. I relived the terrible beatings, the rapes and humiliation. I never spoke of these but Mark and Carol became aware of my emotional problems. My bed-wetting became more frequent and that could not be hidden from their scrutiny. Then of course, there were the many nights I awoke screaming.

Carol in response to my nightly accidents added the laundry to my list of chores. It was impossible for me to complete my homework and my classmates teased me for being so stupid. The teacher had me writing sentences for not completing my homework assignments. To further add to my humiliation, Mike had told everyone at school that I was wetting the bed. I begged Mark to allow me to attend the public schools but he refused. He felt that I would adjust and that the public schools did a poor job of teaching children.

One day in class, Mike told the kids my real name. He mispronounced it but it had the desired effect. Soon my classmates were calling me, Vina. I hated hearing that name; it brought back so many bad memories. I had wanted to bury the past and get on with my life but that wasn't happening. Little Orphan Girl soon became my nickname. I hated that name. My parents were not dead they were just bad parents. I didn't do anything wrong. I was taken away from my family because they did bad things. They lost me! They were being punished, not me. Why did society insist on fixing the blame on me? Even my caseworker Mrs. H would tell people that my parents didn't want me.

Occasionally in class, I would experience a flashback involving something that had happened at my parent's house. Once I saw the watch and its swaying movement when suddenly the teacher snapped her fingers and called my name. My body jerked, an involuntary response, which drew the laughter of my classmates. I sat there in shock, not really knowing what had happened to me. "Down to the office," screamed my teacher! The principal couldn't reach Carol, so this time it was Mark that responded to the school's request to take me home. Mark explained to the principal that I had just lost my family and was having trouble adjusting to my new life. Mark took me visiting that afternoon; he introduced me to some of his family. It was an afternoon devoid of yelling, beatings and chores I had a nice time.

During that afternoon, Mark had explained to me that his parents had divorced and that he had difficulty adjusting to it when he was a child. Although my situation was completely different than his, he became the first person who tried to reach me. He was concerned about the nightmares and started to question me about them. I was ashamed of the dreams and knew if I told him about them, he would blame me just as everyone else did. I just told him, I couldn't remember them.

When Carol arrived home and found I hadn't started my chores, she became extremely upset. Mark had gone down to the basement for something so Carol pulled out the paddle and began to beat me with it. The paddle descended on my back, shoulders and my butt as Carol screamed at me for being such a rotten child. Mark ran up the stairs to find out what was happening. Carol simply turned to him and said, "Veena, called me a bitch!" Mark sent me to my room and attempted to calm his wife down. I lay crying for hours, my body bruised and knowing that Carol's lie would turn Mark's feelings against me. Carol was just like my father had been. She had the ability to make people believe anything she said. Mark grounded me for two days, not that it mattered, I never went anyplace, and the chores took all my free time.

The Easter holiday arrived and Mark bought me the prettiest dress I had ever seen. I was proud to go to church wearing that white lacy dress with its matching shoes. I stood in my bedroom studying my reflection in the mirror, remembering the last time I had worn a white dress. It had been five years ago, on my first day of school. I had grown up so much since then. I still had problems with my feet and the other kids still made fun of me but the loss of my family and my identity far out shadowed those problems. The memory of my life as Vina was fading. It was as if I was blacking everything out except at night when the nightmares came. The situation was terrifying me, in the daylight I was Kimberly and at night I became Vina. What was happening to me? Which one was I? I don't know how long I stood there, wondering who I was before I heard Mark's knock at my door. He called to me, "Are you ready for church, Kimberly?" Lost in thought for a moment, I didn't answer. I hadn't recognized the name Kimberly, when reality sank in I went to the door and opened it.

This Sunday seemed different. The people seemed to be more finely dressed and there was gaiety in the air. Everyone was wishing friends and neighbors Happy Easter. I did not have an understanding of Easter so I asked Mark to explain it to me. Mark told me how Jesus had died for our sins and how he had arisen on the third day from his tomb. "So people can come back from the dead," I asked? "Jesus did Kim. Some people claim to have seen spirits too but I haven't. Have you," Mark replied? I thought very carefully before answering. I didn't want Mark to think I was crazy, after all Kimberly had never seen a spirit, only Vina had. A shudder passed through me. I am Vina! Our spirits are one.

After the church services, the pastor approached Carol and Mark about baptizing me. The pastor thought I should be baptized with my new name. I became furious! I screamed, "I have been baptized. I am still the same person I was before! It's not my fault! Please! Somebody believe me!" The church members just stared; they must have thought that I was crazy. I continued to rant, "If you have been baptized in your spirit, then you are baptized. I am only one person and my spirit has been baptized. I refuse to let you baptize me again!" Then I walked out of the church and went to stand by our car. I watched my so-called new parents as they walked from church. Carol's face was a mask of anger but Mark's beamed with a big smile. Later that day Mark told me that I had displayed a lot of courage in doing what I had done and that he believed in my stance. Carol was furious and believed that I had deliberately humiliated her in front of the church. Like I was supposed to be upset over that? Hurting Carol's feelings was the least of my worries.

School was over for the summer and I was going to have to repeat the fourth grade. I didn't care, I had failed, and I hated the school, my teacher, my principal and my classmates, especially Mike. Mike was considered too young to be forced to do chores, so my workload was doubled, including mowing the lawn. I managed to hurry through some of the tasks, so when Mike went to his friends, I would go to Cindy's house. Sometimes I stayed too long and Carol retaliated by adding additional tasks to my list.

Now cleaning the floorboards in the basement became my latest torture. I hated going down into the basement. Although the basement had been finished off into a laundry and a bedroom, I was still terrified of basements. I was scrubbing the baseboard with the toothbrush Carol had given me when I heard a strange noise. Thinking it was the old man who had died in the pink house my imagination got the better of me? I jumped up, trembling with fear, knocking over the bucket as I ran upstairs.

I went to visit Cindy. While at her house we decided to play with her new Ouija board. We had never played with it before but Cindy knew all about it. We sat on the porch and within minutes I began to sense something was going to happen. I had those funny chills going through me. Cindy and I watched in disbelief as the pointer began to move, Cindy asked softly, "Who are you?" The pointer slowly spelled out the words *VINA'S GRANDFATHER!*

Cindy had no idea, whose grandfather it might be but I did? For the first time since having my name changed, Grandfather was with me. I remained quiet because I had never told Cindy about my past. Something must be wrong, grandfather only showed up when I needed him and here he was. Then the pointer continued moving, tracing out the letters *CATHY.* Chills ran down my spine. Grandpa and Cathy were together. I couldn't believe it. Why? What was going to happen?

Cindy and I were astonished that the game had actually worked. Oh God! What was going to happen to me now? I said good-by to Cindy and I ran home as fast as I could, knowing there was something dreadfully wrong there. I arrived too late. Carol was already home, I heard her screaming as I entered the house. I remembered the overturned bucket and the time I had spent playing at Cindy's. Carol will surely beat me now. My only salvation would be if Mark arrived, but he didn't.

I ran downstairs and found Carol on the floor where she had slipped in the spilled water. Anger glared from her eyes and grabbing me she screamed, "I told you no mistakes. I have had it with you and now you will pay! See what I have found, Kimberly?" In her hand she held the letter I had written Tommy. I had remembered Mrs. Smith's address and written him a letter. Somehow the letter had been returned to Carol's house, probably because I had not placed a stamp on it. I watched her eyes twinkle as she maliciously shredded the letter. Before I could stop myself, I screamed into her face, "YOU BITCH!" I saw the anger flare in her eyes again and felt the stinging sensation as she slapped my face. I was filled with hatred after watching the destruction of my letter to Tommy. I stood there, glaring at Carol, a smile upon my face that could only be described as demonic. In a fit of anger, Carol locked me in the laundry room and went upstairs to wait for Mark to return home.

A couple hours passed before he arrived. Carol explained to him that I had attacked her. She said that the caseworker had suggested, I be taken back to my own home as a means of helping me adjust. Maybe then I would be able to talk about my past life. Mark had his doubts but he believed what his wife told him. Throughout the ride, nobody spoke a word, my heartbeat racing faster as we neared my old neighborhood. The tears started falling down my cheeks as the memories came flooding back. I saw Mark watching me and I heard him whisper to Carol, "Turn around, this is not good for her. Let me try to reach her, you are much to stern with her, Carol. Please let me try!"

Carol kept right on driving and as we rounded the corner, I saw that white, house. Dragging me out of the car and up the walk to the house, my mind numb, petrified with fear, she knocked on the door. I must have passed out because when I regained consciousness, I was being carried in Mark's arms back to the car. I am not sure which of us were crying harder. As I looked back at the house for the last time, I saw Vina's father standing in the driveway. Somehow the luck had gone my way; we had missed him by mere minutes.

Mark cradled me in his arms, consoling me on the way home. I knew that now I had to do something so when we arrived I went into the backyard. I knelt in the grass and silently prayed for what to me seemed like an eternity. I had to end this nightmare that I was living, just how I wasn't sure. I gazed up into the night sky hoping to find the answers. The night chill sent shivers through me so I placed my hands into my pockets to warm them. In doing so my fingers found a small piece of paper. It was the picture I had cut from Cathy's doll magazine so long ago. Now! I knew why grandfather and her had made their presence known at Cindy's. I walked over to the edge of the yard and dug a deep hole. I placed the paper within the hole and started to push the dirt over it. Mark walked up and softly asked, "What are you doing Kimberly?" With no hesitation, I replied quietly, "I'm burying a little girl." Taking a stick I found on the ground I wrote...... *VINA!*

# 8. Chosen Ones

As I walked back into the house, Carol began to speak. She said, "I have made that phone call Mark. It will be taken care of tomorrow morning." I looked into Carol's eyes and saw her joy, she had won her victory but I didn't care. I loathed this woman who had pretended to be my mother. The woman that should have loved and protected me only furthered the torment and abuse I had known.

I walked into my room and started to pack my belongings. I started for the door planning to head north on my escape. Not that I had any idea where north was but I was going to get as far away as possible and my brothers had said they would go north. Somehow, Mark must have sensed my intentions because there he stood in front of the door, barring my way. Mark asked, "Will you at least stay the night? I'll let you leave in the morning Kimberly. Carol has gone to bed, she will not bother you." I set my belongings on the floor, next to the door and I walked over to him. "Thank-you for caring about me Mark. No one has ever cared about me before," I said softly. Mark knelt and tenderly embraced me and said, "I know it is not your fault. You are a very special little girl always remember that. I have been very proud of the way you have stood up for yourself." Then gently hugging me, he kissed me good night.

Mark must have slept on the couch that night. I knew he was making sure that I didn't leave before daylight. For his kindness, I was willing to stay there one more night. Besides it gave me time to plan my new life. I lay there in bed wondering how I would survive on my own, should I try to find some of my brothers? I knew I had no way of locating them so I decided at first light I would search for a new place to call home.

As dawn broke, the sun glowing through the window awakened me; I wanted to leave before the household, especially Carol woke up. To my surprise, both Mark and Carol were sitting at the kitchen table waiting for me to depart. As I approached the door, I noticed my belongings were missing. Carol noticed my confusion and said, "You arrived here with nothing and we bought you those clothes but you will leave here without them." This angered Mark, who yelled at her saying, "We cannot wear any of those clothes Carol. She can have them and some of the toys. After all, I bought some of them for her." He went back into my old bedroom and packed my bags, returning with more than I could possibly carry.

I sorted through my things and picked out only those that I thought I would really need. As I turned to depart, I heard a knock on the door. At the door stood Mrs. H, she had come to remove me from my first adoptive home. I did not want to leave with her; I wanted to live by myself. I had no luck when it came to my relationships with adults or parents.

I watched Mrs. H's eyes as I slowly walked to the door. I wanted to escape but she remembered what had happened months before and grabbed my arm and said, "You are not going anywhere missy! You are in deep enough trouble now. Just try and run away and I'll have the judge lock you up for a very long time." She turned to Mark and Carol and explained, "I knew she would be trouble, the very moment I first laid eyes on her." After she escorted me out of the house and into the car, she started her usual lecture about how hard it was to find me a home. How I should be grateful for all I had.

I lost it then, yelling loudly at her, "I have nothing to be grateful for. I have scrubbed on my hands and knees for hours, in exchange for my food. How many ten year old girls do you know of that do that?" Startled by my outburst, Mrs. H attempted to respond saying, "It is not my fault that your parents didn't want you, so stop yelling at me." The pent up hatred spilled forth, "My parents did not give me away, they lost custody! MY GOD! My father raped me, tried to hang me and forced me to have sex with strange men so he could get drinking money. Do you have any idea how that feels? Do you? How would you like to live like that? Don't you understand? My parents didn't take me to the shelter; the police came to our house and removed me and my brothers and sister. We were abused and in danger. Would you be able to adjust to living with strangers after that? I am a little girl, I have feelings, why can't you understand that?"

Clearly shaken by my revelations, Mrs. H said, "Vina, I'm so sorry. I cannot imagine what it was like to live like that. I had no idea, that you had suffered such hardship. But you have to go." Without thinking, I suddenly remarked, "Vina's dead. I buried her yesterday. My name is Kim." That really startled Mrs. H, who lost control of the car, having to swerve suddenly to avoid an accident. She regained control of the car and pulled to the side of the road where she asked me, "What do you mean, Vina's dead?" I replied to her question, "I was confused about who I really was. Sometimes I was Vina and other times I was Kim. Am I crazy Mrs. H? Do I need to see a doctor?"

"No," she replied, "But you have to understand that we changed your name for own your protection. The judge felt that your father would be upset with your testimony and he would try to harm you. We didn't want him to be able to find you and hurt you." "What should I do if I see him Mrs. H?" I asked. She replied, "You must run and hide. You can never see your parents again." "You know, he'll kill me if he ever catches me," I said back to her. She looked at me sadly before she replied, "That is why we changed your identity because Vina was too uncommon a name. You must never tell anyone your true identity. It is for your own protection remember that. Quietly I asked, "What about my brothers and my sister?" Her response was, "They have all been placed in good homes. You are the only one left. You are becoming too old; it is harder to place older children. Vina, I mean Kim, if this home doesn't work out, I don't know what will happen to you."

"What are they like Mrs. H? Do they know that I am not pretty, that I am not very smart and that I don't always speak correctly?" I asked. Mrs. H answered me in a soft voice, "They have three other children and they want one more. They seem to be a very nice family. When we get there, please try to smile; I've never seen you smile. Also try not to say any words with a *S* in them and of course walk slowly." "I did smile, when Tommy and I had our picture taken. Is Tommy still my brother? Why can't I see my brothers and sister? They won't hurt me. Why don't these people take all of us? If they like kids so much," I replied. "There were too many of you and besides the others are all placed with nice families now and living normal lives," she answered me as she pulled into a driveway. I quietly asked, "What's normal?" Looking at the red brick house, which was to be my new home, she replied, "Something I hope you can find here Kimberly." All the old fears came back to me, only this time ten fold. What would they expect from me? Why did they want an unintelligent, ugly little girl for their daughter? I tried so hard to keep my feet straight but my knees were shaking so badly I almost fell. Mrs. H grabbed me, preventing my fall and helping me to regain my balance. "Try a little harder, she is watching you," Mrs. H said. Knowing that the person, who would decide my fate, was observing me walk, only contributed to my nervousness. Before I could stop myself, I tripped and fell onto the sidewalk. I hurriedly stood up, praying I hadn't been seen.

Suddenly the door opened, I just knew the woman had seen my fall. Why else would she be smiling? Oh God! I know she won't want me now. With my head hanging, I entered the house and walked into the living room. There were toys scattered about the floor and three children laughing, as they played. It was the picture of a happy family and suddenly I was jealous. This was something I could only dream about.

I looked about the room, the couch and chair matched, unlike the ones in my parent's old house. This house reminded me of somewhere I had been, but I couldn't remember where. The colorful pictures on the wall, lent comfort to this home. That's it this house is a home! This home was filled with love and support. This was something unlike anything I had experienced in any of the homes I lived in previously.

I stood quietly as Mrs. H talked to the woman. "Her name is Vina but the other family changed it to Kimberly. If you like, you may change it to something else. She failed the fourth grade but she really has been put though quite a lot these past months. We are hoping that a loving family can turn her grades around. Her lowest grade was a D+ but that was enough to fail her in the school the other family had enrolled her in. She has some problems with her feet turning in but I believe that can be corrected. She also mispronounces some words but she is a pretty little girl and she works real hard." My mouth must have dropped a mile. What had they done to my caseworker? This was nothing like the introduction she gave to Carol, five months ago! Mrs. H was actually saying nice things about me.

"What would you like your name to be?" the woman asked. "You can be Vina or Kim and if you would like a different name, we can change it to something else." Mrs. H quickly interrupted her and explained that the courts did not want me using my original name and I stated that Kim was okay with me. At that point in my life, I did not want to unbury Vina. I needed time to heal. My mind had blacked out most of the bad memories and I allowed only a few memories from my previous life to linger. The memories of my brothers and sister were the only ones that Kim would share with Vina. Then again, I must not forget Grandpa; somehow I knew he would not let me forget him.

Mrs. H said good-bye and once again I was left standing in a living room wondering what to do. What did they expect of me? Should I sit on the couch? It took just a few moments for the lady to realize how afraid I was. In a pleasant voice she inquired, "What do you have in your bags?" I sat down on the floor and started pulling my toys from one of the bags. I was shaking with nervousness and I dropped one of my Barbie dolls. She quickly picked it up and called to her daughter, "Clare, see what your sister has." The little girl in the corner approached slowly, taking one or two steps at a time. The other two children were boys and they had no interest in my dolls, they only stared at me.

The woman turned, pointed to the little girl and said, "This is your sister, her name is Clare. We adopted her when she was three days old. The two boys on the floor are your brothers. Their names are Joseph and Francis. They are seven and eight years old. We adopted them four years ago. Now my family is complete, I have two boys and two girls." The woman slowly turned to show Clare one of the dolls from my bag. "Why don't you come over here and play with your sister, Clare?" she asked. Clare only stood staring shyly at me. The lady continued to speak, "They look like they are brand new." I replied softly, "I didn't play with them often." The truth being, that I didn't have time to, with all the chores I had to do at Carol's house. Most of the toys that Mark had bought for me to play with still remained in their packages.

I timidly asked, "What's your name?" She bent down onto one knee and replied, "Mom, but you can call me by my first name, which is Phyllis, until such time as you feel comfortable calling me Mom. The man in the picture, is your father, his name is Joe. He's at work right now but will be home later." Phyllis went into the kitchen and made a couple of phone calls. She seemed very excited about something. I wasn't sure what it was but it had arrived this morning. I listened to their conversation for a while. I really wasn't, eaves dropping because I didn't know what else to do. The other children were just sitting there watching me. I didn't want to cause a scene and even though they were getting on my nerves, I ignored them.

I was feeling extremely uncomfortable so I began to look about the room for something to help me relax. I was very careful not to look at the three onlookers. I studied the pictures hanging on the walls. Two of the pictures caught my eye. One being a large black and white portrait of Phyllis and the other picture was a man. I studied these pictures for a long time, hoping to tell from their eyes, what kind of people they were. For some reason I could not tell if they were nice people or not, why couldn't Kodak capture the image of a soul on film? I stared at the pictures for a few moments longer. I wished I could determine if the man in the picture was like my new mother in the kitchen. For the moment, I had to wait until he came home from work.

Startled by a knock on the door, I jumped. That brought about laughter from the children in the other room. I wanted to find a place to hide, thinking that Mrs. H had returned to take me to another home. This house seemed so different from the others I had been in, everyone was happy. My new brothers and sister were just like me. They were adopted too!

As an older woman entered the house, my new siblings swarmed over the lady hugging her. She turned in my direction and said, "Hi! I'm your Grandma Jo. What's your name?" When I first tried to answer her, I was tongue-tied and couldn't make a sound. This older lady had overwhelmed me with her cheerfulness. She continued to smile and in a few moments I relaxed and responded by saying, "My name is Kim." Then Phyllis came into the room and said, "Hi Mom, I just got my new daughter." Much to my surprise the older woman replied, "Well, she fits right into the family."

Shortly afterwards, Grandma Jo left to go to work and once again the room became silent. My stomach was still a tangle of uneasiness and I had developed a headache. The other kids were still intently staring at me and Phyllis seemed preoccupied in the kitchen.

So once again, feeling alone and afraid I stared at the pictures on the wall.

Suddenly another lady came out of a bedroom giving me a questioning glance. She said something that I couldn't understand because it was a language I had never heard. I stared back at her not knowing what else to do. Phyllis laughed and said, "Don't worry about her Kim. She's harmless. She is very close to Clare and right now she thinks that Clare won't play with her anymore. Don't be afraid, she'll get use to you."

The old lady sat in a chair and like the others began to stare at me. That is everybody but Phyllis. I looked around the room trying to ease the trembling of my heart but now even the pictures on the walls were staring at me. I just couldn't take it any longer, the tears I had tried to hide, had their way. I didn't want them to think I was a crybaby but I couldn't hold them back. I had no safe haven to escape to, so I buried my face in the sofa cushions and cried.

Phyllis heard me crying and came in from the kitchen. She picked me up in her arms and carried me to a rocking chair. We rocked back and forth. Sitting in her lap made me feel so comfortable, not since that night with grandfather, had I felt that way! Trying to soothe me even further Phyllis said, "If you feel like talking about what you have lost, I will try to help you overcome your pain, Kim." Then she told me how they had come to adopt the other children. She and Joe had not been able to have children and so they had adopted their family.

In her arms I felt the love and support I had been missing in my life. As she gently rocked me in her arms, I could sense there was something different with this woman but I could not explain what it was. She seemed to care for so many people. The three children, her mother and the old lady who didn't like me, all loved her. Why couldn't this woman have children, she had so much love in her heart to give. Instead, God enabled people like my real parents to have children they didn't want. Was this fair?

We sat there rocking in silence, neither of us making a sound. I with my long brown hair, curled within her lap resting like a babe in her arms. The room was so comfortable, the atmosphere so peaceful. It was a dream come true, a home, a family, both offering love and comfort.

I am not sure how long we rocked in silence but after a bit she whispered, “I love you.” Startled I replied, “You can’t love me, you don’t know me!” She answered softly, “Yes I can Kim, because I chose you. The mothers that can have children naturally are forced to love and care for whom they give birth too. They are stuck with them. God let me pick my children and I’ve picked you.”

# 9. I Find A Dad

While Phyllis was rocking me in her arms, I started to relax and regain my composure. Although the three other children were still staring at me, the knowledge that they too were victims made me realize that they understood what I was feeling. They were no longer a threat but they were equals, children who had been unloved, not wanted and separated from their birth families. Somehow, Phyllis made all that seem unimportant. She was a substitute mother, a person who took what other mothers had not wanted. She wanted me, for the first time in my life somebody wanted a dark haired, pigeon toed little girl instead of a blue eyed, blonde haired baby. Somehow that realization filled me with hope. She was so different from other mothers, she was kind and loving and I felt so safe and comfortable in her arms. At that moment I knew I had found a home.

I remained on Phyllis' lap until she felt certain I had relaxed and was comfortable with my new surroundings. Then she simply asked, "Would you like to get to know your brothers and sister? They are very excited to have you here." I got off her lap and began to look around her house. "I'll show you around Kim, here let's take your stuff and put it in your bedroom," she said. We walked down the hallway and stopped at a large bedroom with a full size bed in it. "This is your sister Clare's and your bedroom," she continued speaking, "You can put your belongings in here." I placed my things on the bed and waited for further instructions. I was expecting a list of chores but there were none forth coming. So I turned and followed as she showed me each room of the big three-bedroom ranch, I was to call home.

This was still strange to me, not knowing what was expected of me. I followed her into the kitchen where there was a sink full of dirty dishes. I didn't like doing dishes but I wanted to do something special for her because she had done something nobody had ever done for me before, she had said the words, I Love You. I shyly asked, "Would you like me to wash the dishes?" Her reply shocked me,

"Only if you want to Kim, you don't have to. I know some kids don't like doing dishes but if it makes you feel better, then go ahead." I walked over to the sink and started to do the dishes. As I turned the faucet on I heard Phyllis say to the other children, "Help your sister with the dishes." They slowly made their way into the kitchen, I had not expected any help but I felt better knowing that I would not have to do all the work.

I had hardly begun to wash, when Joseph voiced his objection. Francis and him were not going to wash dishes! Clare said she would wash or rinse but she would not dry them. Suddenly Joseph splashed water on me and before I knew it, the four of us were engaged in a water fight. We were laughing and fighting with each other behaving just like a family of happy kids. We made quite a mess of the kitchen but Phyllis didn't seem to care. The distraction caused by the water fight helped me to unwind and feel totally at ease with my new family. Soon, I was outside playing in the yard with my new siblings. I was free to be a child, running, laughing simply enjoying life. This was something I'd only dreamed about and now it was happening.

We played outside for hours and before I knew it I had forgotten that I was in a strange location. That is until the sound of Phyllis' voice brought me back to reality. "Come in and get cleaned up for dinner," she said as we all trooped into the house. "Dad will be home in a few minutes so get washed up," she continued. The realization that I had yet to meet my new father filled me with dread. I thought, what if he doesn't like me, will this dream be destroyed? Was this just a fantasy I had been allowed to experience?

After washing up for dinner, I went into the living room. Not sure of what was allowed, I sat on the floor. "Sit by me Kim," Clare called from the couch. I got up and went to sit next to my sister. I was nervous about doing so remembering that it wasn't allowed at Mrs. Smith's. Yet, Phyllis seemed to make a house into a home not a fashion statement. Although she kept a clean house, the furniture was for the use of the entire family, even the children could sit on the couch when they wanted to.

However, when Phyllis came into the room, I jumped up and asked if it was all right to sit on the couch. She laughed as she replied, "I didn't buy it to look at. It is for everybody to sit on, that is what a couch is for. I buy things for my family to use and you are part of this family Kim." It wasn't long before I heard someone coming to the back door. I could tell it was a man's voice so I knew that my new father was home from work. Fear of the unknown, gripped me once again. What if he doesn't like me? Where would I go? So again, I stared at his picture on the wall, praying that God would give me the strength to make it though the rest of this day.

When my new father to be entered the kitchen, I could hear him talking to somebody but his words were not clear. So I leaned forward and listened intently, he was not speaking English. Oh No! What have I gotten myself into now? How will I be able to obey him, if I can't understand what he says? All of the thoughts and fears came flooding back, paralyzing me. Suddenly! There he was, standing in front of me. Just how much does God expect a ten-year old to handle? Surely I had surpassed my limits long ago. Yet somehow or the other, I always found myself in the same situation, waiting to see if somebody wanted me. Will fate intervene today and allow me the home I've prayed for? A home where an average little girl will be wanted or will I spend the rest of my life doomed to wander from house to house? The decision now rests with the man who stands before me.

I stood there in front of my new father feeling like I was an item of clothing on a clothes rack. There are so many to choose from, perhaps he will want to shop around. Is the outfit too small or the wrong color? Will he grab a different one? Maybe if he appears undecided I could tell him that the sale hasn't been finalized and that I can be returned. Of course, unlike clothes, I can grow, I can change the color of my hair, perhaps I'd look better in a different outfit, I'll go change into one of the others I brought with me. I watched as he bent down and knelt in front of me. I tried to smile like Mrs. H had told me but my face refused to cooperate. All I could manage was a simple grin. Slowly I moved my eyes up to see his. I thought if I looked deep into his eyes, I could tell what was in his heart. I gazed for a mere moment or two before I had realized this man was the dad I had been looking for.

He slowly turned to his wife and said, "She has beautiful long hair." Phyllis replied, "Yes, but its kind of thin." It took everything I had but I mastered a big smile. "Please keep me," I prayed, "I have nowhere else to go." I wanted to say something in my own behalf. I swallowed hard, opened my mouth but once again my voice betrayed me. No words came forth.

I closed my eyes and began to imagine what it was like being a normal child. I remembered playing in the yard with my new siblings, the running, the laughter and the uninhibited fun. There, in a span of hours I had been a kid. At that moment I decided to be thankful for whatever decision they made because without even knowing it they had given me something I never thought I'd have. The chance to be a kid.

I opened my eyes at the sound of silverware rattling. Phyllis was setting the table and my new dad was reading the evening paper. The other children were watching a television show. Surely somebody must have seen me staring off into space or had time stood still? I wanted to ask if my dad knew if he was going to send me back with Mrs. H but I did not remember what Phyllis had said his name was. How should I address him? Before I could speak he asked, "Are you hungry Kim?" I nodded shyly. "Wash your hands then," he replied.

As I walked into the kitchen, I noticed an empty chair. Pointing to the chair Phyllis said, "This is your seat." I sat down quietly and picked up my fork, watching how the others were eating. After my stay at Carol's my table manners were much better, but still! I noticed that nobody was chewing their food thirty-two times before they swallowed. Nobody had their napkins folded neatly on their laps and everybody was eating together at the same table. "Weren't the men any better than the women?" I wondered. In my new home the women could eat together with the men.

I glanced around noticing everybody had a full plate. I could remember when watered down bean soup was considered a feast, my only real meal. Now upon my plate were meat, potatoes, and a vegetable. This was more than I could eat, if in fact I could eat at all, my stomach was still tied in knots. As I played with the mashed potatoes on my plate, I listened to the table talk. The kids were talking about the television show and planning tomorrow's adventures. My new dad was talking about work, although I didn't understand all the words, it was evident that he had incurred a hard day.

Suddenly grandma had entered the room and began to speak to him. He replied to her in the same language, they had used earlier. I was so relieved that he could speak English; at least I could understand him. I had never met anyone before that could speak two languages.

It wasn't long after dinner, that my first day ended and most importantly I had survived. Phyllis had me sleep in a smaller bedroom that night because of Grandma Anna's jealousy of me. I remembered Phyllis telling me that she had been very close to Clare. I had heard her complaining earlier but couldn't understand the language she spoke.

That night I went to bed feeling a little afraid, alone and having an empty feeling. I had lost VINA and missed her dearly but I needed to bury her if I was to survive. The pain she had endured was much too great for me to bear besides I thought she was losing her mind and that was the only way I could keep my sanity.

I lay awake for hours wondering if I would last at this home, about my birth siblings and about what kind of people would want four children that were not theirs? Images began to float across my eyes, Vina begging for food, Vina being beaten, Vina having her innocence torn from her. As I lay alone and scared in my darkened room, I began to think of my life as a jigsaw puzzle. Some pieces fit without effort while others wouldn't go into the boundaries. The mountains in the scenery were much to high to climb but one day I'd reach the top and seek out my lost family. The river's raging currents washed away the paths so for now I must follow my heart. The sky offered hope, much like what my new family did but neither of them made any promises. The red cabin in the picture with its rusty doors presented a far more difficult challenge. Some of the pieces could fit different places just like my memories. They could be shuffled around from place to place, fitting the forgotten areas that time had blackened out.

Of course, there were some pieces that didn't seem to fit anywhere. Perhaps time is needed to heal those areas and then someday I'll unlock the secrets behind that rusty door. Maybe then I'll discover what really happened to a little girl named Vina!

I awoke in the morning still filled with uncertainty. I lay in bed listening to the other children laughing over a cartoon show. They seemed so happy and their laughter seemed to be infectious. Was it healthy to laugh so much? Could it cause a heart attack or a stroke? In the end I thought, what does it matter because what good is living if one cannot enjoy it?

"Yaba-daba-doo," yelled Francis as laughter erupted from the living room. He was the hyper one and seemed full of life. Although his impression of Fred Flintstone was poorly done, I had laughed at his attempt. Suddenly I heard footsteps coming down the hallway, Phyllis must have heard me laugh. I hid my head under the blanket, hoping she wouldn't see me. As I peeked from beneath the blanket I saw her standing there. I feared the worst because I had sinned; I had laughed out loud and would be made to pay for it. Carefully she pulled down the covers and softly said, "Getup sleepy head. It's time for breakfast. Do you like cartoons? The other kids are watching the Flintstones so come out to the living room with the rest of us."

I strolled out to the living room where the rest were lounging about on the floor. "What kind of cereal would you like," Phyllis asked? Fearful that I would pick the wrong one, I answered, "I don't care." She listed several kinds that she had in the cupboard, including Lucky Charms. I picked Lucky Charms it was my favorite cereal. Carol bought it for her son Mike and occasionally I would be allowed some. Not often though because Carol said it cost too much and I was only to eat the lesser quality cereal. That was when I was allowed to eat breakfast.

I finished eating the Lucky Charms and went into the living room with the other kids. I felt like I had died and gone to heaven. Maybe I was dreaming and still asleep. I had a meal before I earned it, surely this wasn't going to last. I know that cereal is not a gourmet meal but to a child that had to beg for food and eat out of a dog's dish, cereal was just as good. Besides, Phyllis had given me my favorite without even hesitating.

After everybody ate breakfast, Phyllis told us to go outside and play. She didn't have to tell me twice. I was going to be a kid for as long as she let me. I swung as high as the sky on the swings and slid so fast down the slide. I hid myself in the fort and played war with the others. I played tag in the yard and ran as fast as I could when suddenly I tripped over my feet and fell to the ground. For a moment I thought my dream had ended. Then without warning, Joseph approached from behind and yelled, "You're-It!" They, didn't even laugh at me falling, the game went on.

After playing for hours, we rested on the lawn. They had five acres of property and although we had certain boundaries, the yard was so huge and they had a swing set, a play tractor that you could ride on and more toys then I ever imagined could exist. Yes, this must be what heaven is like I thought. As I lay on the ground resting, I looked to the sky and said, "Thank-you God. This place is truly a dream come true and if it ends tomorrow, please let me find a way to say thank-you to the people that allowed me to be a kid. Oh! One more thing God, could you let Vina see through my eyes? She deserves the chance to be a kid. Amen."

Shortly after that, Phyllis called us into the house for lunch. Two meals in such a short span of time I'll get fat I thought. How could people eat so often? Still, maybe Vina might be watching and will get mad if I turn food down, so I better eat. I ate as much of lunch as I could but I could not finish my sandwich.

After lunch Phyllis sat down beside me. "I noticed you have trouble walking Kim. Is it because you are pigeon toed?" I felt my heart in my throat and swallowed hard. I couldn't answer. Was my dream home ending? Would I be forced to continue the search for somebody to want me? It had been, to good to be true after all. "Have you seen a doctor?" she asked. "Yes," I replied, "Mrs. H took me a year ago." "Well, I think I'll make you an appointment and see if we can get them corrected and while I'm at it, I'll wash your hair and try to make it thicker." Phyllis said softly. I looked up at Phyllis, to say thank-you, but I had been caught totally off guard. I could not hold back the tears; they were not sending me back because I had bad feet or too thin hair. Instead, they were going to spend their own money to correct my feet and my hair. I only hope I prove worthy of their efforts.

When Phyllis saw my tears, she asked if I felt like talking about it. I only shook my head no. I was not ready to disclose my pain. I had buried my past and that is where it belonged. Phyllis interrupted my thoughts by saying, "My boys have the same birth mother and they also have a sister. We didn't want to split the family up but the little girl was already adopted. Do you have any brothers or sisters somewhere?" I replied, "Yes." "Well, when you feel like talking about it, I promise I will listen. Always remember this, anyone can be a mother but not everyone can be called a mom. I don't know how your birth mother treated you or any other mother you may have had. I will always be here when you need me no matter what Kim." When Phyllis had finished talking she sent me out to play with my sister.

Afterwards, Clare and I played with some toys in the living room. I heard Phyllis make an appointment for me at the doctor's. Then she had called Mrs. H and asked if I had any brothers and sisters? I could tell from the conversation that they had all been placed in permanent homes. At that moment I realized that they were not looking for a perfect little girl, they just wanted another daughter whom they could love. Perhaps they are strange, because there are not many people like them. I had gotten lucky. From that day forward I referred to them as my Mom and Dad. I knew that no matter what my flaws were, we would be able to work through them. After all, people can learn from their mistakes, especially if you have loving parents to guide and protect you.

Just as mom promised, I was taken to a foot specialist. This time the specialist wasn't paid for by the courts but rather by my new parents. After my examination, he fitted my feet with braces and ordered special shoes. He stated that this condition was normally treated at an earlier age but that there was still hope that my feet would respond to treatment. During the summer of 1970, I adjusted to living with my new family. I think that knowing we were all adopted helped tremendously. We were all equals, with nobody being treated special. Everybody had to help with chores and be responsible for the cleanliness of their rooms.

Unlike my previous families, my new parents had many friends and relatives who visited often. Although everybody was friendly, I had a harder time adjusting to having company around the house. The memories of my father's friends lay deep within me. Those faces that had tormented Vina still haunted me. Someday no doubt, I'd learn to trust people and would not close them out but for now I remained withdrawn in my shell, with my buried feelings.

Many people bury their feelings, often with out even realizing it. Vina had hid under the table, keeping a safe distance from those that meant to harm her. Kim used a shell. She built barriers to her heart. These barriers forged a safe haven, allowing no one to enter and no one out. Undoubtedly, the loss of my loved ones played a significant role in that decision. Uprooting me from my home, the loss of what belongings I had i.e. clothes had been one thing, the enforced separation from my siblings who had shared so many traumatic moments, had only left me filled with unbearable pain. I treated those people who attempted to reach me like the puzzle pieces. I scattered them about never really placing them into their proper places. Until I felt capable of showing love, thesc barriers would stay in place and I would remain in my shell.

As the summer progressed, I was no longer concerned about having to work for my food, clothing or any other items I needed. I was treated as a member of the family and I learned to enjoy the many things that other kids took for granted. During that summer, I remembered back to the time that Vina had cut the picture of a doll out of a magazine just because the picture had showed a girl smiling. Now I had plenty of dolls but their smiles no longer mattered. I had discovered that smiling wasn't a sin. It was our emotions that made us human and nobody had the right to deprive another of that.

Near the end of August, my mom and Grandma Jo took all of us kids shopping for school clothes and supplies. Grandma Jo spent a lot of time at the house and I grew very fond of her. Unlike the shopping trip with Carol, this was a shopping spree I enjoyed. I was allowed to pick out my own clothes, express my personal choice, something I had never been allowed to do before. All of us were permitted to buy an outfit for each day of the school week. Afterwards we went to a restaurant for lunch. This time I wasn't hid in a corner. My mom wasn't ashamed of me. We enjoyed our meal and laughed about our first shopping trip together.

After we finished our meal, we went home and showed dad all the outfits we had purchased. I was startled when Grandma Jo said she had spent all her money but her last dollar. I knew that one of the outfits cost a little more than the others and wondered if I should have picked out a cheaper one. I instantly offered to return some or if necessary, all of them. I could do without. I always had before. I was so surprised when Grandma Jo took her last dollar from her wallet and asked my dad to fold it. She placed the folded dollar into the back of her wallet and said, "This dollar shows how much you mean to me Kim. I will never let this dollar go. There are some things that are more important than money. I think you are one of them Kim. So promise me that when I die, that you will look in my wallet for this dollar."

September soon arrived and with it the start of the school session. Although I had failed the fourth grade, my parents enrolled me into the fifth grade. Both they and the school officials felt that my unstable home life had played a significant factor in my grade point average. The fifth grade proved very challenging for me and I had an extremely difficult time with reading comprehension and vocabulary. I was placed in a remedial reading course and a special speech class. With hopes of increasing my comprehension level and word pronunciation, my teacher struggled hard to help me overcome my handicaps. Whereas today, one hears about the Sylvan Learning Centers and the Hooked on Phonics programs, in the seventies there were few programs that offered hope for children who suffered speech and reading problems.

My interaction with my classmates had improved over that from the other schools. The students no longer made fun of me but I still kept my inner most feelings under lock and key. This time I isolated myself, keeping the few friends I made at a safe distance. Still somewhat withdrawn and shy with people around me, I chose to watch life pass me by. I had my safeguards in place, which left little room for interference. I would not allow myself to be hurt anymore.

One of my classmates in the fifth grade was also withdrawn and shy. I remember the first class that she attended. She had to stand up in front of the class and recite her name. The name was uncommon and the kids all laughed at her. Everyone but me, I remembered the way Vina had felt when people made fun of her name. I became angry and stood up, yelling at my classmates to shut up. The teacher was somewhat shocked at my outburst but quickly got the class under control. During the recess period, our teacher pulled both of us aside for a talk.

The new girl sat near the teacher and explained that she had recently been adopted. She continued to say that she felt so alone. She had been given the choice of changing her name but had decided not to; since it was the only thing she had left. I was so proud of her when she stood up and declared, "I have been stripped of everything. You can not possibly understand!" I saw the hurt in her eyes and I felt her pain. I wanted to reach out and help her but I did not know how.

Maybe if I had shared my pain with her, I could have helped her but I wasn't ready to let down my barriers. So I simply apologized to my teacher and walked out of the classroom. I sat on the swing and recalled the fear I felt when I first met my mom and dad. The feelings the new girl expressed surfaced within myself and I felt my tears start to fall. I watched the other children running and playing. They had no idea of what life was really about. That life could be so full of pain and sorrow. Looking up at a nearby tree, I saw the wonderful colors of fall. The leaves in beautiful hues, as the sun cast a subtle glow upon the branches flickering in the breeze. I was momentarily comforted by this display of Mother Nature.

A year ago I was at Mrs. Smith's living with Tommy, earning our room and board by doing housework and other jobs. It had been a day similar to this one, when I had begged the judge to allow us to stay together. That day seemed like a million years ago. So much has happened in one year. I remembered hiding his shoes, as a means of getting even for some prank he had pulled on me. Now, I'd give anything to say to him, "I love you." Oh God! How much I miss him. Why did they have to separate us? I never said good-bye, I had wanted to be brave and not cry in front of him. If I could only turn back the clock to that farewell, I'd tell him how I really felt.

Swinging back and forth, I looked around the playground and noticed that except for the new girl and myself; it was empty. The rest of the kids had returned to class. I hadn't notice her standing there until she said, "I'm scared." I simply replied, "We're late." Neither of us spoke about our hurt as we walked back to the classroom. If I had shared the tragedy of my life with her, I might have helped her but I was not strong enough yet. However, without knowing it she had helped me, I had learned a valuable lesson, one that I carry in my heart even today. No matter how much you might be suffering, there is someone out there carrying a greater burden. So I stopped feeling sorry for myself and decided that someday I would help someone the way she helped me.

That night, as I lay in my bed, I could recall the look of pain in the new girl's eyes. Her pain made me realize just how much my life had changed in a year. Some of my pain had been cleansed from my body in the short time I had lived with mom and dad. The love and understanding they demonstrated daily had helped to erase some of the horrors of my youth, allowing me to enjoy my childhood.

That year my dad enrolled me in band class. The other band members had started in fourth grade so I had to work hard to catch up with them. I was using dad's coronet and he worked with me often, ensuring I learned the proper notes and techniques. Sometimes I'd just listen to him play and I could tell that he really enjoyed playing the instrument. So, I practiced every night hoping that I would make him proud of me. After several months of practice, I participated in our first concert. It was a Christmas concert and we played several Christmas carols. Our band sounded terrible but like everybody's parents, both mom and dad said we sounded good. I was amazed that they took the time to point out several things they liked about the music. Never once did they point out any of the flaws.

With Christmas fast approaching, my parents started to decorate the house. They had a huge tree filled with different colored ornaments and lights, just like the one I had wished for many years ago. Sometimes, they even drove us around different neighborhoods, so we could see the pretty Christmas decorations. During our scenic tours, dad would talk about Santa Claus and how he left toys for all the good little boys and girls. "Do you believe in Santa Claus, Kim?" I was asked. I only shook my head no, after all, there should have been one year that I had been good enough to have received a small gift.

One night they let us stay up to watch a Christmas special. We turned off all the lights and lay on the floor to watch the show. The only lights that lit up the room were the television screen and the lights on the tree. As the bubble lights flickered against the darkened walls, shadows from my past danced before me. Suddenly I was five years old again and standing in front of my father as he lit the match to that homemade tree of Christmas past, destroying all hope of Santa Claus as the tree melted before my eyes. I could smell the burning paper and feel the stinging of his slap across my face. I stood up ready to run for my safe haven and it's mice, then I heard dad ask, "Are you okay Kim?" I felt foolish when I realized where I was. So I simply said that I had to go to the bathroom.

When Christmas Eve arrived, there were dozens of presents under the tree. Dad loaded the car with several of them to take to relatives and we eagerly went to our Grandparent's house to have a Christmas party. I had never been to a Christmas party before so I was a little apprehensive. All of our aunts, uncles and cousins were there; the house was filled with people, Christmas decorations and the festive holiday spirit.

It wasn't long before gifts had been exchanged and people reminisced about Christmas's past. Now I was once more feeling alone and isolated. Last Christmas, I had been with Tommy, wards of the State. Now, I have a new family. My mind blacked out the scene before me and flashed back to a time I had been with Allen, Bob, Betty, James, Tommy and Chiefy. I wondered what they were doing this Christmas, if they were happy and if they had found families like mine.

Soon I was back in the present, listening to the laughter. The Christmas spirit seemed to get more boisterous as the evening wore on. I believe the liberal use of spiked eggnog, might have played a major factor in the festivities. Although the drinking of hard spirits was allowed, nobody had consumed excessive amounts. If only my father had learned to control his drinking, maybe I would still be with my birth siblings. Instead I am in a crowded room, feeling very much alone. I still felt out of place and I wanted to hide but having no place to go, I sat on the couch beside Uncle Howard. He sensed my discomfort and engaged me in small talk; before I knew it the evening had ended.

On Christmas morning dad told me to follow him downstairs. As we neared the bottom of the stairs he said, "I know you don't believe in Santa Claus but the other kids do. I want to show you something that you got for Christmas. I didn't want you to be disappointed, because I don't think you have ever had much of a Christmas. Your mom and I wanted to make it special for you this year. The pink one on the end is yours," He pointed to four new bikes as he continued to talk, "I stayed up all night putting them together. Merry Christmas, Kim."

Of course there were still some gifts under the tree, but the best gift of all wasn't wrapped nor could I ride it. It was the two people standing in front of me, who cared enough to pick up the pieces, when a strange little girl needed it.

It wasn't long after Christmas that my adoption became finalized. I was now legally their daughter. I belonged. In the six months I had lived with my new family, I became a kid, a human being with emotions, who had started to love again. There are no perhaps! This is why I choose to call these wonderful people my Mom and my Dad. I love you, too!

# 10. Smart Enough

Life with mom and dad only became better. I learned the joys associated with being a child and most importantly I learned that I did not have to fear men. My dad is one of the most understanding men I have ever met. He treated me with respect and never raised a hand to me. I was punished when I deserved it. Sometimes I was grounded but never again was I subjected to a physical beating. I had my assigned chores but never more than any normal child could be expected to perform. They both felt that an education was extremely important and they encouraged me to prepare for college. I could not have asked for more helpful parents.

I think the most devastating thing that occurred that first year I was living with my new parents involved my hair. My mom had decided to curl my hair and it became very snarled in the rollers she was using. I had to sit in the chair for a couple hours while mom tried to clear the tangles. Several times she apologized thinking she was hurting me as she tried to untangle the curlers. Having experienced more severe treatment than this I didn't cry but my mom did.

It wasn't too long after that happened, that mom took my sister Clare and I to the beauty salon. I loved my long hair so when it was cut extremely short; I was devastated. The only thought in my mind was that my dad would send me away because I no longer had long beautiful hair. When we arrived home, I went straight to my room and placed a hat on my head. I refused to remove the hat until after dad came home from work. I finally removed my hat and waited for dad to pass judgement on me. "It looks pretty Kim," he said, "It will grow out again and this time it will be thicker and prettier."

After that I never again worried about being sent away. The night before my adoption was to be finalized my mother told me they had no regrets about choosing me and were very happy having me for a daughter. Then she asked me if I wanted to spend the rest of my life with them? I did!

As the months passed I learn to cope with many of my fears. The passing of time had allowed some of the memories to fade but there were still obstacles I would have to overcome. These obstacles were to form my journey through life, that pathway leading from childhood to that of an adult woman. They loomed before me as a mountain might and like a mountain it would prove hard to climb. Many of the trails would lead nowhere.

One such tear filled trail was caused by the loss of my birth brothers and sister. The family that was so casually erased by the Michigan court system left many scars on my heart. However, I learned to love and cherish my adopted family and they helped to fill the void left in my life. I vowed to find my biological brothers and sister and opening the doors closed by the courts would prove to be an almost insurmountable challenge. I knew the odds were stacked against me because I had buried the person they knew as Vina and the courts had removed all traces of her identity.

Everyday the blackness of my early youth turned a lighter shade of gray. The nightmares that once filled my twilight hours became less frequent. The burial of Vina had helped enormously but the abuse that shattered my youth still haunted me on occasion. Only when I became older, did I come to understand what had happened to me.

It was about the time I turned twelve that I began to realize what my body had been subjected to and I became filled with hate for the man called father. I was sure that the court had imprisoned him for the crimes he had committed against his family but that hadn't stilled all my fears. I still felt a need to hide when I was in public places or when I was in a room full of strangers. Even with my new identity, I was always afraid that my father would discover my whereabouts so I seldom wandered off alone.

Most of my outside activities involved the church and school. One day while attending a local church with my family, I chose to wander around the church grounds after Sunday school. It was a lovely summer day and I waited for my brothers and sister at the church bus. The presence of the bus driver gave me a feeling of safety so I strolled about the lawn looking at the beautiful flowers. I had only been walking for a short time when I heard someone yelling, "Vina! Vina!" I turned to see who it might be, when I realized what name they were calling me. I knew that I was in danger and I turned to get help from the bus driver but he was no longer there. I ran for the bus and hid beside the tires. As I peeked around the front of the bus, I saw them standing there. It was Bob and my birth father. I was shaking with fear, knowing that my father would kill me, if he could catch me. He continued to call, "Vina! Where are you?" I stood up seeking to run and escape when the bus driver returned and opened the door. I ran up the steps onto thc bus and hid behind the seats at the rear until the other children had gotten onto the bus. As we drove away, I glanced out the window and saw that piercing look in my father's eyes and I realized I must never relax my guard again.

When I returned home, I told mom that I had seen my birth father and brother at the church. She seemed surprised that my brother would be with my father and stated that I might have been mistaken. Mom seemed concerned but she felt that my birth father had been denied visitation rights to all his children. He would be in contempt of court should he ever make an attempt to contact any of us. I lay in bed that night wondering why he wasn't sent to prison. At the trial, it had been determined that the abuse had indeed occurred. Why was Bob with father? Bob had been the one to call the police. After all those years of abuse that led to the trial and the destruction of our family, why did Bob go back to him?

The doors that were closed just a few years ago once again swung open and the memories once more flashed before my eyes. The pain I had felt years ago threatened to overwhelm my senses. Somehow I was transported back to when I was five years old. I stood shaking with fear before the man called father as I relived the horrid events leading to and culminating with the trial. I tossed and turned for hours as I struggled against the memories of physical and sexual abuse. Eventually the flashbacks subsided for the night. The abuse had ended when my family adopted me but the nightmares and the flashbacks would continue to haunt me.

Exhausted from my nightmarish struggles, I went to the window seeking solace amongst the stars. They seemed so tranquil and peaceful, clouded in the morning's mist as if they were wearing a veil. Perhaps the answers I sought were to be found in those mists. I remembered the incident that had led to my hanging. Surely my testimony about father's evil perversions would result in a more grisly death should he ever find me.

Still terrified, I closed my eyes hoping that the flashback would disappear. This usually didn't work but this time it did. The image of my father and his eyes brought forth many questions, which just seemed to run together. Why was my father so abusive? Why were the people who tried to help me so ineffective? What had I said to the judge? How much of the sexual abuse had been omitted from the testimony? Why was the struggle to find loving parents so difficult? Why must I continue to live in fear?

The memories seemed vague and unclear. In fear of my life I had not told everything about the abuse. There had been sufficient evidence produced to substantiate the testimony that father had routinely withheld food, physically assaulted and sexually molested his children. The results of my medical exam alone should have convicted him. Instead of him being imprisoned, his children had been sent away. The crimes he had committed had been erased as easily as they had stricken the name Vina from existence. He too could have found another family. Another family to beat and sexually abuse because society with its justice is blind mentality had given him another chance.

I knew the testimony about the physical and sexual depravity we had endured had shocked the judge. However, when I told the judge to have me killed rather than being sent back to suffer a slow and painful death at the hands of my father stunned him. I had not been given access to any professional counseling although I do remember talking to the black robed judge in his chambers. Much of what I may have said remains shrouded in mystery. Those records were sealed.

The medical exam I had been forced to endure substantiated that I had been repeatedly sexually violated. My father had allowed his friends and even strangers the use of my body. Most of the men that father had forced Betty and I to have sexual intercourse with shall remain nameless. They were never mentioned at the trial and they too, were able to walk away from the crimes they perpetrated on us. I did not want to re-live those past events so I just named all the people who had sexually abused me *FATHER!* After all it had been my father who had enabled all them!

I sat up in bed with my mind racing and my heart pounding like a drum. The memories of the trial had only brought back more pain. It was that pain I had chosen to bury with the little girl named Vina. I decided that it didn't matter what had been disclosed at the trial. I knew that the testimony was so damaging that my identity had been changed to protect my life. Most adopted children do not have their names changed including those with uncommon first names. One of my classmates had been allowed to keep hers but of course the circumstances surrounding her adoption had not been as harsh as mine.

As the morning finally arrived, my mind wandered down another path. Was father looking for me? Would I have to live in fear of my past forever? I now knew what it was like to be loved and to live as a normal person, one who was free to think and speak what was on her mind. My dad had spent a lot of money having my feet corrected and I now walked without the braces. I was exhausted but determined not to act like anything had happened. I began my day much like any other. Mom and dad never mentioned anything about the events of the previous day nor did I share the anxieties I felt as a result of my father's appearance.

Saturday night arrived and I began to wonder if father would be at the church. What should I do? I would pretend to be sick so that mom would keep me home. I awoke much later than normal the next morning. Mom and dad had not awakened anyone. Instead they decided to take us to visit my grandmother. When we returned, mom told me that they had decided against sending us to that Sunday school and would find another church to attend. They would take no chances with my father being able to find me.

I decided I needed a way to let out some of my pain. I secretly began to write about the little girl named Vina. The journal contained all the details of her life that I refused to share with anyone. It was extremely personal in nature and served a two-fold purpose. First it enabled me to vent some of the anger and hostility buried within me and secondly I recorded the details of those flashbacks that were occurring. Someday in the future I would need this knowledge.

I continued to write in my journal for several months. Each entry disclosed feelings I wanted hid from the world around me. Although I still struggled with a reading disorder, causing the passages to be poorly written, I felt my journal was serving the purposes I had intended. Many were the nights I struggled to find the proper words to convey my memories. Some of them were fading away such as what age I had been when I was first raped.

I wrote page after page detailing my father's control compulsion and his use of hypnotism to control his unwilling victims. Had I actually become a sexual zombie or was I so convinced that he could do anything that I had just closed my mind to what was happening to me? I swore that nobody would ever own me the way my father had. I would take charge of my own life and no one would ever make me do anything I did not want to. I would never again become anybody's toy.

My journal contained some things that remained a mystery to me. Like missing pieces of a puzzle, there were areas where I just wasn't sure of what had happened. Time after time I asked myself, "What could I have done to change my life? Had there been a way to stop the rapes? Could I have avoided the beatings? What had I done that was so terribly wrong?" I had always felt that what had happened was my fault and I had deserved whatever punishment I had received. For those many months I wrote about the brutal details that existed only in a file stamped *CASE CLOSED.*

Although I had kept my diary well hidden in my bedroom, I always feared that someday somebody would find it and read what I had written. That fear became a reality on one day. I was outside playing with my brothers and my sister Clare had remained inside. Somehow she had discovered where I had hidden my journal and had read most of, if not all of my entries. I was devastated and once again felt violated. The two of us had always shared our belongings so Clare really had no idea that she had done something wrong. She never mentioned anything about what she had read. Perhaps now she will understand me. I decided that it was no longer safe to continue my journals and destroyed them. How much easier would have it been to write this book had those journals still been in existence?

Once again the guilt from my past threatened to overwhelm me. I no longer had an outlet and the pain became an enormous burden to bear. I tried to keep busy doing other things such as band. I enjoyed playing the coronet and I practiced for hours in the evening. Mom and dad enrolled both Clare and I in ballet classes. The doctor had thought that it might help strengthen my feet so we attended classes once a week. Every time I tried to stand upright on my toes, they would cramp severely causing me an unbearable agony. I was undoubtedly the worse dancer in the class.

After months of practice the day of our recital finally arrived. The hall was packed and there were all those strange faces in the crowd. God! What if father was amongst them? I hated being out in public. Although mom and dad were in the audience I still felt fearful, afraid that something might happen. Dancing in the front row only heightened my fear of being seen by my father. What if he saw me with Clare? Would he harm her as he had threatened to do with Cathy? I swore to myself that I'd not let anything happen to her. I was the one he wanted and I would sacrifice myself to keep her from being harmed. Clare did not need to suffer the indignities I had.

After a couple years of dance classes both Clare and I moved on to other things. I joined the Girl Scouts and there were several activities that kept me busy. I loved camping in the woods because there I was out of the public eye and I felt safe enough to let down my guard. In the scouts I also went roller skating, attended the theater and participated in arts and crafts.

During one of the scout outings I attended a local movie. I cannot recall the title but afterwards a pastor had requested that those members in the audience that wanted to be saved to come forward. Most of the girls in my troop went forward but I remained sitting in the back row. I was too afraid to go forward and confess about the sins that tormented me all those years. I sat there alone lost deep in thought. If there was a God, why had me put me through this hell? Why did I have to ask forgiveness from a stranger for the sins God had allowed?

I watched the other girls in my troop finish their confessions and leave. Suddenly I had an urge to go to the front of the theater where a few people remained with the pastors. I slowly walked to them and remained quiet not knowing where to begin. How could I tell complete strangers about the ordeals I had suffered when I refused to tell those dearest to me? I knelt beside the pastor wondering how to begin when suddenly from out of my mouth came the most sordid details of my past.

As calmly as discussing the weather I told them about my life as Vina. I spoke of the beatings, my starvation and the rapes that left me filled with shame. Then I mentioned how I had buried Vina and my fear about father discovering my whereabouts. Before I realized what was happening I had all the pastors cloistered about me crying as they prayed over me. I looked into their eyes and asked, "Am I going to hell?" The men just stood there dazed and bewildered so I asked my question again, "Am I going to hell?" One of the pastors knelt beside me and answered, "No! Why would you think that you would go to Hell?" I replied, "My father told me I would because of my sins." The pastor paused before continuing, "You do not have to worry about the sins your father forced upon you. I think he has a place in hell waiting for him. It is his sins that need forgiving. Do your adopted parents treat you well?" "Oh yes! They love me," I quickly responded.

Those few moments of confession enabled me to close the doors on guilt and concentrate instead on getting along with my life. When I turned sixteen I took a job as a waitress. As a means of overcoming my fear of public places I chose to work in the public's eye. My first day of work was dreadful. I cringed when people tried to talk to me. I longed for the table I used to hide under as a child but I forced myself to stay busy and the evening was soon over.

I worked a lot of hours during the next couple of days and actually started to enjoy working with the public. I had met a lot of friendly people and some of them were my age. In fact one of the cooks asked me out on a date. He was an attractive man and very polite but there was something about him that disturbed me. I refused his offer. A couple days later Jim asked me out once again. I continued to turn him down. The next day I went to work determined to find out why I felt the way I did about him. I couldn't find him because he had quit the restaurant and joined the service. After work I told my mother about the strange feelings I had when I was in Jim's presence. She asked me if I thought that he might have been my brother? Although it had been years since I saw my bothers, I felt sure that I'd recognize them. Wouldn't I?

Later that day I sat on the porch trying to picture what my brother Jim might look like. He would have been the same age as the cook. The odds of running into my brother had to be very high. Surely the judge had spread the family over the county when he had separated us. Could I have attended the same school as my brother and not have known it? My co-worker had a different personality than Jim who was reserved and shy. The cook had been out-going and very friendly. What might have happened if I had dated the cook and he had been my brother? Might I have fallen in love with him and once again committed a sin with a relative? I was determined that I would not date any men who might be the age of my brothers without first asking them if they had been adopted.

It's funny but now as I reflect back, I can recall some good times but back then there was nothing but evil. With tears in my eyes I recalled how Jim had taught me how to fight. We would wrestle for hours on the blacktop that served as our prison. I remembered when I once hid Tommy's shoes and I laughed for hours as he searched for them. He hadn't thought it was funny but then I had always hidden things from him. I realize now that was my way of getting attention. Then there was my big brother Allen who walked us younger children to and from school. Father had made him drop out of school to watch over us. He did so unfailingly. Little Chiefy must be all grown up now. Someday little brother I will find you. My hero was Bob. He had rescued all of us from that hell never suspecting the price that would be paid.

I felt the wind blowing across my face as I stood up and walked across the yard. The tears were falling down my face and I needed the time to compose myself because I didn't want anybody to see me crying. Yesterday at school I had been asked if I had a sister and without thinking I said yes thinking they had meant Clare. They said that they had seen my twin on the other side of town when they were shopping. I asked them exactly where they had seen her hoping that it might have been Betty. I had hoped that the judge would have shown us some mercy and placed us sisters in a family together. After everything we had gone through, together we might have been able to console and help each other. It had been seven years since our separation and I would not know where to start my search.

Suddenly I heard Clare calling out my name. I turned to ask what she wanted and she replied, "You must be a million miles away Kim. I've called out to you several times!" I simply answered, "I was daydreaming Clare. I thought I was somebody else."

Not long afterwards I started to talk with my Grandma Jo about my birth brothers and sister. I told her that I still missed them and that I wondered if my mom and dad would be upset if I looked for them. She said that she didn't think they would get upset with me as long as I did not contact my father. She asked me if I knew how to go about searching for them and I told her I had no idea as how to conduct a search.

I told her how some things were blocked from my memory and that I was afraid of what I might find. I continued talking about how I looked at my past as a mountain with all it's difficult paths leading to the top. Grandma asked, "Why do you picture it that way Kim?" I described a memory of putting a puzzle together with a person who described the journey that way. I couldn't remember who it was but I thought it was my dead grandfather. She smiled and asked, "When did you last see him Kim?" I replied, "The day before I came to live with Mom and Dad. He disappeared when I buried Vina."

Grandma hugged me tightly and said, "Kim, you will climb that mountain someday. It's only superstition and don't let anyone stop you. Those pathways are filled with obstacles to scare you and you mustn't let them. Besides you have almost reached the summit. You have survived an extremely abusive environment; you attempted suicide, testified against your parents, lost your siblings, buried yourself and talked with your grandfather's ghost. Now my dear, what can be more frightening than all that?"

Less than two years later I was graduating from high school. I had put on my cap and gown and sat beside some of my friends. The crowd consisted of families and friends of the graduating seniors. During the speeches and award presentations I found myself wishing that my birth brothers and sister could have been here as I walked across the stage to receive my diploma. After the ceremonies concluded, I watched the graduate's families come forward with hugs, kisses and flashing cameras. My loving family was there too but something else was missing. Yes! I wanted scream to the heavens, *Mrs. H! I MADE IT! I even have the paper to prove it.*

Someday I will confront my past and seek what is rightfully mine. I have many questions that I want answers for. The most important being, how or why did father escape punishment for his horrendous crimes? The courts owe my family an answer. One day I shall ask the man who wore that black robe those questions only this time I shall be in front of his desk not underneath it.

# 11. Rock-a-bye-Baby

After the graduation ceremony, I went out with a guy whom I had been dating and we discussed growing up. It wasn't until that moment that I realized how much my life had changed. I too, had taken things for granted. Such things as the movies, ice-skating, roller-skating and dinner at the local restaurant had all become a part of my life. Mom and dad had given me a chance to enjoy life and somehow over the last nine years I had become a normal person.

Now as an adult, I could walk straight and I no longer needed the braces. My teeth had been corrected a couple of years ago and I now had a healthy body. At that moment, I realized that I had always tried to deal with my past or analyze it. Now it was time to look to the future and bury the past.

Statistics labeled me as a person that would become a bad mother, probably unsuccessful and more apt to commit crimes. However, my outlook of the future was entirely different. I saw the past as those things in life that I could not change but the future was not set in stone. Determined to prove the statistics wrong, I enrolled in a nursing college. Although my grades had improved enormously, my reading comprehension level was still low. After failing the entrance exam, I enrolled in a nearby junior college. I passed everything but reading. This time however, I spoke with a coordinator who placed me in a special reading class.

Within days of my acceptance to college, my parents held my high school open house. Many of my relatives attended the party. Our house was packed with family members from my adopted family some of their names I was not even sure of. The fear of people that had once overwhelmed me had been exorcised many years ago. Now as in adult, I no longer looked through the eyes of a child. Somehow over the last nine years, I had overcome some of the obstacles of my past. I no longer jumped when a stranger spoke to me; I had a steady boyfriend and a future that I was determined to control. Although one day I vowed to find the siblings I once knew, I now sought to find the answers that every normal person asks of himself. What do I want out of life?

As the next several weeks unfolded, I prepared for college and the man I had been dating proposed. Although we planned to marry later in life, our relationship had developed like that of most young adults into more than just holding hands. At this point in my life, I questioned my own womanhood. After all that I had been though, I was not sure that I could be a wife to anyone. Still dealing with flashbacks, nightmares and many buried skeletons, I decided to tell my fiancée about some of the abusive past that I had endured. After several tearful hours spent discussing my childhood many of the questions that I had buried inside me, were unleashed.

Before the evening was over, I no longer worried about my ability to be a woman. However, after a few short months the outcome of that night came back to haunt me. Because that evening had transgressed into something neither one of us had expected we didn't take precautions and I became pregnant. Terminating my pregnancy was never an option for me, because the child I carried was now a part of me.

At first, we decided to move our wedding date up and hide the pregnancy but the issues of bride maids and invitation to our families brought back painful memories. I desperately wanted to share that moment with the siblings from both, my adoptive and birth families. However, that was impossible because now I was pregnant and time was running out.

We decided to discuss our problem with the pastor at the church I attended. However, I was too embarrassed about the pregnancy, therefore we decided to meet with the pastor from my fiancee's church. After disclosing all the details of our problem, we decided to elope. The pastor had agreed to perform the ceremony within a couple of weeks as long as we attended marriage counseling with him. Which gave us time to get the blood work completed, decide on a place to live and get our marriage license.

A local doctor had done the blood work, which in the seventies consisted of checking to see if you had any diseases and if you were blood related. Afterwards, we found an apartment that was close to both our parents. Now all that was left was the marriage license, so one afternoon we drove over to courthouse. Slowly I walked to the entrance of the building. Surely filling out a simple form should be easy enough. There was only one problem. It was the same building I had spent countless hours in many years ago. Now as I neared the front of the building, images from my past appeared. There beside me stood Mrs. H, looking at me with that look of disgust on her face. Without even realizing it I had entered the courthouse. Now, as I looked down the hallway, I could hear Mrs. H saying, “You are not that bright, your feet are bad and you are not a very pretty little girl.” Why hadn’t I ever screamed, “That even the ugly girls have a right to live?” I had been judged, sentenced and convicted by the same court that probably had let my father go free. After all it had been easier to sentence me rather then place him behind bars. Someday I will seek out the truth and find out what the judge had done with the man called father.

Within a couple of days after filling out the forms for the marriage license, my dad received a phone call while I was working at a local restaurant. It was my fiancee’s pastor, apparently his wife had gone into labor and he would have to postpone the marriage counseling. Of course, now that my adoptive parents knew of our plans to elope. Those plans were abolished. Within days of my parents finding out, preparation for a small wedding took place.

After the wedding, my parents invited everyone to a nearby restaurant for a reception dinner. As the dinner was being served, many stories about growing up with my adoptive family were discussed. Before the meal was over, I found myself wondering whether I would have survived if the court system had not intervened.

However, now that I was married, that part of my life no longer mattered. Beginning my life as an adult came easy for me. I could always relate better to adults than to children. Perhaps I had grown up a little faster than other children, who were the same age as me. I was now married, my childhood was over and I was determined to concentrate on the future. I had a child to think about and a new husband. Now was not the time to deal with the past. It was the time to prepare for my unborn child. A child, who would be loved and cherished, from the moment he or she was born.

It was only a couple hours later that I stood in front of what was now to be my new home. Only this time I had picked it out. Although small, it was a place that I could grow to love. My adoptive parents, who did everything to make this day special, purchased most of the furniture. We even had a rocking chair for the baby, when he or she arrived.

Life as a married woman was easier for me than I had expected. At first, I feared that I would suffer more flashbacks because of our sexual relationship. However, that never caused a problem. My new husband always understood and never did anything against my will. As a matter of fact, prior to our marriage he had promised to help me search for the brothers and sister that I had lost so many years ago.

Our marriage was just like any other young couple starting out. We both attended college and worked full time but money was always tight. We had a lot of expenses and as the pregnancy progressed we now had medical bills too. But no matter how tight we were I loved the fact that I would soon be a mom and hoped that this child would fill the void in my life. However, by the time I had reached my fourth month of pregnancy, I started to have the same reoccurring dream over and over again. During this dream, I saw my body lying in bed, a foreboding mist throughout the room and a telephone. There was another person near me but I wasn't sure who it was. As soft music played in the background, I tried to listen to the lyrics of the tune but the words were unclear. After a few minutes, I began a conversion with the mysterious person. He disclosed the fact that I would have a female relative die in the near future, but before her death occurred, I would need to make a phone call. I attempted to pick up the phone but it was out of reach.

Each dream left me puzzled as to who the person was. All I knew for sure was that I loved this person more then life itself and would have given up my life to save hers. Selectively, I started to search for the mystery woman. There were only a few females in my life that I loved more then life itself. My first thought was my adopted mom and sister who lived down the road from me. If the phone did not work in my apartment, I could simply drive over to see them. So I ruled them out. There was my birth sister Betty but I had no idea whether she was alive or dead. Therefore, I would not be able to call her. Finally there was Grandma Jo, who had moved to Arizona. I would have to call her. So I knew it had to be her. I phoned her twice a week but had no idea what I was supposed to tell her.

After two months of this ongoing dream, I still had no idea of what I was suppose to say. I feared the possibility that I would not find a way to reach the phone and say whatever I needed to tell her. Determined to change the outcome, I sought answers concerning any medical issues that my grandmother may have had but found nothing of a serious nature. Exhausted from the stress, I begged the spirit to disclose more details. However, the same dream tormented me night after night. With no new clues and still not sure who the mystery person was, I started to have cramps that were so severe that I was rushed to the hospital. After several hours of medical attention, the doctor released me stating that I was just paranoid.

As the month of January approached, I started to lose weight. The dream occurred more frequently. Now several times a night, I awoke startled and confused. While my questions remained unanswered, I sensed an end was drawing near. I knew the phone was the key to my mystery and realized that my phone looked nothing like the phone in the dream. But what puzzled me even more was the fact that Grandma Jo's did not look like it either. So now, who was the mystery female?

By January 7$^{th}$ I was exhausted from the sleepless nights so I retired early. The dream confronted me as soon as sleep overtook me but now everything was brighter. The mist had gone, leaving a clear vision of the phone and the room around me. I traveled through the doorway of a darkened hall only to see nurses standing by a desk. In search of the phone and the female in danger of dying, I floated towards another room. There, I wasn't allowed entrance.

Then suddenly I could see the spirit floating towards me. I should have been terrified but I wasn't. Without warning, I felt myself moving backwards. I glanced behind me and saw my body lying on the bed and within a few minutes the blankets reclaimed my chilled body. Dazed and confused from the out of body experience, I sought answers from the spirit that remained by my side.

As I turned to speak to the spirit, I saw him slowly disappear and from out of the darkness, his voice echoed these words, "It's time." I jerked my body into a sitting position to ask what he meant by "It's time?" Then I saw the bed covered with blood and at that moment, I knew my unborn child was the female in danger of dying. Within minutes I was rushed to the hospital. Although my first instinct was to panic, I was determined to change the outcome of the events that had been disclosed in the nightly visions.

After several hours of labor and medical attention, I delivered a beautiful baby girl. Weighting less than one pound, she was rushed from me immediately. Due to the fact that I was only 24 weeks into my pregnancy and her low birth weight she was placed in a special unit for premature babies. After her birth, although I was exhausted from the labor, I begged to see her. I desperately wanted to hold her. However, her lungs had not sufficiently developed and they had to place her on life support. I asked one of the doctors when I would be allowed to see her and he replied that I had lost a lot of blood and thought it would be best if I rested for a few hours. Then he turned and wrote something on a pad of paper. Within a second or two, he handed me a phone number. He told me I could call and check on her any time.

When I arrived in my room, there wasn't a phone. I asked to be placed in another room where I would be near a phone but there were no other rooms available. The nurse on duty stated that the hospital was remodeling this wing because of the new neonatal unit. The area across the hall from me was cordoned off. They were remodeling that area to construct a new labor and delivery unit, so the mothers of premature babies could be closer to them.

A few hours later, the nurse on second shift took me to see my newborn daughter. Although I could not hold her because she had wires everywhere, I managed to touch her tiny hand. She was so small but yet so perfect an every way. Her body was fully developed, from her dark hair, down to her tiny toes. She was just like a baby doll. I watched her laboring to breathe, saw the smile as I rubbed her hand and the eyes that looked up to me. I prayed that God would give her a chance to breathe on her own and the strength to survive.

I sat with her for hours, as she struggled for life. The harder she labored to take a breath, the more helpless I felt. I wanted to help her but didn't know what I could do. I had always had a safe haven but now there was nowhere. I had to face the possibility that once AGAIN I might lose MY family. I had bonded with a daughter whom I loved more than life itself.

Slowly I walked out of her room and into the long hallway. There was a lot of construction so I followed the detour signs around to another corridor. Not sure of where I was, I wandered into a room with a cross. There I knelt down and prayed for my daughter, whom I knew was dying. It was then, that I deciphered the key to my nightmare. MY GOD! The telephone! I knew the call I had to make but there were no phones. I started to run down the hallway as the vision appeared before me. It was the phone, the spirit and the same hallway I had entered many times before. Everything was flashing before my eyes, as if I was watching a black and white television set in slow motion.

I tried to think of where the phone was in the vision. Slowly I focused on the objects around me. I closed my eyes, in an attempt to see the vision more clearly. It was in the nurses' station. When I opened my eyes I was laying on the floor in the hallway. A couple of people were trying to help me. Regaining my composure, I started to walk down the long hallway. The faster I walked, the longer the hallway became. I started to lose my balance again and I saw a couple nurses running for me. As one nurse grabbed me she said, "Your as pale as a ghost. You lost a lot of blood yesterday when you hemorrhaged. You need to rest." Weakly I replied, "I need to make a phone call." At first, the nurse told me to rest for a while, then I could make a call but I knew I had to make that call quickly. So I replied, "I need to call a pastor for my daughter. I want her baptized before it's too late." "It's snowing hard and it's almost 8 P.M. I doubt that you will get a pastor here tonight," the nurse said in a sympathetic voice.

The other nurse ran and retrieved a wheelchair. I grabbed the phone book and looked up the phone number for the pastor from the church I attended while I was growing up. He answered within a ring or two. I told him I delivered a premature baby and did not think she would survive the night. He simply responded he had not been good enough to perform my wedding ceremony, so he refused to baptize my daughter. I reminded him that I was still a member of the church and my husband had been recently confirmed there. His response shocked me. *"Call me in a week or two... if she lives that long."* I slammed the phone down. I started to turn but my body wouldn't move. Something was wrong but I wasn't sure what. I looked down as my hand shook on the receiver. The phone....Oh God.......the phone. It was the same phone in my dream. Frustrated, confused and scared I screamed out loud. GOD, HELP ME! I watched in disbelief, as the page turned in the phone book. There in the middle of the next page, were numbers that stood out because they were so bold and bright. I wasn't sure of the pastor's name, I just knew that it was the pastor that I needed to reach.

It rang a few times before I heard the voice on the other end. It was the pastor that had recently married me. Although we had chosen to attend services at the same church my adoptive parents attended, I hoped that he would not hold that against me. I quickly explained the situation about my daughter and to my surprise he arrived at the hospital within a half an hour of the call. As he wheeled me down the long hallway, I told him about my reoccurring dream. Suddenly he stopped and asked, "Is your daughter's name Jennifer Renee?" "Yes," I said. He remarked, "I had a vision last night concerning a phone call. The man on the other end of phone stated that I would receive a phone call tonight concerning his little granddaughter. I was waiting for the call when you phoned."

I looked deep into the eyes of the tiny baby watching me as the pastor baptized her. "I love you Jennifer," I cried. She no longer had the strength to squeeze my finger but I knew she understood. Her eyes told me so. It was the first time I saw the pastor cry. Both of us stood outside the doorway and cried like babies for several minutes. After he regained his composure, the pastor told me that no matter what happened to my little girl she would be taken care of. That she must have had an angel watching over her because his vision was the strongest he ever experienced before.

After the pastor left, I laid in bed praying that she would make it though the night. When sleep finally came, I was again tormented by the same dream. However, this time when I saw the vision it was so true to life, it terrified me. The dream now detailed the faces around me, the hallway was brightly lit and a desperate feeling to overcome the odds. But what terrified me even more, was the melody that played loudly in the background. *Rock-a-bye-baby.*

When I recognized the tune, my body jerked. There at the end of the bed, stood an old man holding my newborn daughter and I knew it was to late save her. As I stood on the cold hospital floor, my mind heard these words. *Bye-bye mommy.* But I wouldn't accept that so I ran out of my room and down the hall. The nurse on duty grabbed me and said, "Where are you going in such a hurry?" "My daughter just died! Please, I want to see if they can bring her back." I saw the other nurse at the desk put down the phone. The look in her eyes told me that it was true. My daughter was gone. She had died the moment I awoke from my dream.

All the nurses on duty refused to take care of me. I was labeled a witch. So I lay in bed, crying over the baby I had so desperately wanted. After several hours my doctor entered the room and told me that when my vitals were stabilized I could go home. Then he asked questions about my medical history pertaining to childbirth difficulties in my biological family and any injuries that could have caused me to go into premature labor. It was at that moment that I realized that my past might have caused the death of my daughter.

Her funeral was small. I stood in front of a tiny casket that held a baby who never had a chance to live, just like John Calvin, the brother that died so many years ago. It was then, that I realized I had to research my past. I needed to know my medical history and I wanted to find the siblings I once knew. Perhaps Betty had the same problem. Maybe, premature births ran in my family. I wasn't even sure if I had been born premature.

As I knelt down and placed a rose on my daughter's grave, I promised her, I would find out WHY this had happened. I never had that dream again but every once in a while I hear the haunting lyrics to *Rock-a-bye-baby.*

# 12. Promises I Keep

From that day on I vowed to leave no stone unturned. Although I was not sure where to start my search, I had the benefit of knowing the birth names of the people I was looking for. Most adoptees searching for their biological families have no knowledge of who or what they are looking for. I had the names of my siblings and their ages. However, I had to face the fact that at least two of my brothers could have served in the armed forces during the Vietnam War and they may not have survived.

When I first started my search I went to the county clerk's office and filled out an application for my original birth certificate. However, there was no valid birth record. After questioning the clerk, I was informed that the proper procedure was to petition probate court for my records. So immediately I went to the probate court building. At first I thought the court system would allow me access to the siblings that had reached the age of eighteen. So when I made contact with probate court for the very first time I felt confident that I would receive the help I requested. However, that was far from true. During that time frame the adoption laws were very restrictive. We had very little rights. Most of the laws protected the birth parents and governed what little information we could receive.

After filling out the form I handed the paperwork to the clerk handling records. As she glanced over the paperwork I thought I saw a questioning look in her eyes. Since I had never met this woman before there was no reason for her to be upset with me. Still I felt uneasy about her. Perhaps she had been involved in the trial many years ago or maybe she was just having a bad day.

I waited impatiently after she left the room in search of the records. Many thoughts entered my mind. Hopeful I could be reunited with my lost siblings. I found myself wondering what do you say after all these years. What if they don't like me? What if I don't like them?

After a few minutes she returned to the room and stated that the file was in the attic and the person named Vina had died many years ago. The undertone in her voice told me the clerk was not very receptive to adoptees searching for their lost love ones. Still I pursued information from the clerk stating that I needed to know medical information. But this inquiry was rebuffed also, leaving me with no recourse.

I left the courthouse feeling empty inside. A part of me wanted desperately to walk back in the building and ask her why I was denied medical information but instead I chose to wait a week or two. So I drove around the neighborhood where several of my old classmates said they saw a person that looked like she could be my twin. Hoping to find someone that looked like Betty, my husband and I drove around for hours. Feeling lost and depressed I even went in search of Carol and Mark's old house. After hours of searching, we reached a dead end and my husband and I returned home to our apartment.

The first few months of my search left me feeling violated and alone. So I sought answers from a group that claimed to assist an adopted person searching for knowledge. Although this group appeared to be helpful to most of the members, it left me feeling even more isolated. My quest was different from that of the usual member. They were either searching for the birth parents that had relinquished their rights when they gave birth or the child they had chosen to give to a loving family. I knew both my birth parents' and birth siblings' names. My quest was searching for the people they had become.

As the meeting drew to a close, some of the members indicated that my search was much easier than theirs after all I had names and the knowledge of why I was given away. They had nothing to go by. But I didn't feel lucky. I had a lifetime of nightmares, flashbacks and feelings of guilt that left me wishing I had died many years before I had reached this meeting. Perhaps none of us were lucky and then again maybe I just didn't fit into this group.

It wasn't long before I returned to probate and the search for my past. But again, the same clerk stood behind the desk. I watched her handle others seeking information from their birth files and she appeared to be professional in her efforts. However, when it was my turn to stand in front of Mary, I saw the expression in her face change. She did not like me for whatever reason. But I wasn't going away! I wanted answers. I was tired of being the victim. So this time I was prepared. When she stated that Vina was dead and that I had no rights to her file, I screamed, "Then give me her death certificate. I want to know what she died of." I watched as her face turned white and her mouth dropped open. But she responded quickly. "That file is in the attic and that is where it will stay as long as I am alive. The past is over, leave it alone no one is searching for you."

But I couldn't leave it alone. I was pregnant again and I wanted medical information. This time Mary had indicated that she had checked the file and found no medical information. So again I left feeling like all the doors were closed. Shut out from the world around me I returned to the school I attended when I was living with my birth parents. As I walked down the long hallway of a brightly lit building I approached a stairway that entered to the second floor. Slowly I climbed the stairs as all the students returned to their classroom. At first their screams echoed down the hallway. Then somehow the noises around me blended into the walls and the hallway changed to a black and white scenario. The year was now 1969. I was bruised and scared as I stood in front of the teacher explaining how I had fell and injured three fourths of my body. Of course I was lying. I had to.

I felt a sudden jerk of my shoulder and heard someone calling, "Kim." It wasn't long before I realized I had suffered a flashback. It was time to leave. I was in no condition to subject myself though this much pain. Searching for medical information was one thing but indulging in the past, which left my body shaking with fear was another.

So during the rest of my pregnancy I chose to leave the past alone and concentrate of my unborn child. But it wasn't long before I had a glimpse of the future. In the form of a dream in which I saw a beautiful blue blanket covered with different hand stitched animals. I searched many stores to find the blanket in my dreams but was unsuccessful. So I purchased the materials and mom showed me how to do embroidery. I worked hard to complete the blanket before the birth of my second child. However, by the time I reached my seventh month, I hemorrhaged again.

After hours of labor I delivered a son weighting 2 pounds 9 ounces. Although the odds of his survival were slim I believed my dream was an indication that he would survive. I never gave up hope. However, because of his premature birth he had difficulty breathing and he was placed on life support. After I was discharged Jeff remained in the hospital struggling to survive. I spent hours at the hospital watching him and taking pictures just so I could compare them to the day before.

Then one night we received a telephone call. Jeff was having complications. The doctor did not think he would make it through the night. While we were waiting news of Jeff's condition we knelt to the floor and prayed. At that moment I prayed to the Lord and asked him to spare my newborn child. If he would grant me this one wish I would teach him to love God. Then I did something I never thought I would do. I asked God to forgive my father for the sins he committed. At that moment I had released all hatred in my heart and forgave the man called father.

Within moments of my prayer Jeff's condition had rapidly improved and after sixty-nine days of hospitalization we were able to take our son home. I never had the dream of the blue blanket again. However, Jeff spent many hours of his youth under the little hand-stitched animals that I believe was a sign of his survival.

It wasn't long before I started my search again. This time when I went to the courthouse, I requested records that were available to the public. I remembered my births parents having marital problems before the family had separated so I decided to see if they had applied for divorce. Court records had revealed that my parents had petitioned the court for divorce in January of 1970. All seven of their surviving children were listed as permanent wards of the probate court.

It seemed odd looking at all our names on their divorce papers. They even listed our birth dates. I carefully glanced down the list. Although I still remembered everyone's age, I wanted to make sure my memory had not become flawed over time. After calculating the approximate year they would have graduated, I went to the pupil accounting service that dealt with the school district we had attended before our separation. They were able to trace where everyone had been transferred to. However, they did not have a record of their new identity.

I at least had an idea of where everyone had attended school. It surprised me to find out that two of my brothers might have graduated from the same school that I had. But there was no hope for Chiefy because he had never started school before the family separated. So I had to face the fact that he might be lost forever but never forgotten.

There was no other information listed on their divorce papers. It was very cut and dry with no property, no alimony and no children to fight over for custody. They both had the chance to walk away and start anew. The address listed for my birth mother was incorrect and neither of my birth parents had listed phone numbers. Although I did call a lot of people with the same name, it proved to be a dead end.

I drove around the areas where my siblings had attended school. However, all but Tommy and Chiefy had graduated. There was the possibility that they did not stay at the first home the courts sent them to. They could have been sent to several foster-care houses during the trial and then sent to permanent homes afterwards. Which means they could have been relocated to a different state. But still I searched those areas they might have been relocated to. I even went through my husband's old yearbook. Because he had graduated from the same school I had only four years earlier he might have attended some classes with my brothers Bob and Jim.

I frequently visited probate court during that year. However, each trip was unsuccessful and Mary's attitude became worse. I realized that the court system had taken me out of that environment as a child because of the abuse. However, I no longer looked though the eyes of a child. I was not searching the past to obtain revenge. I was seeking medical information and the whereabouts of my lost siblings. We had been victimized in the past and I still felt like I was being victimized.

However, I was determined to locate my birth siblings no matter how long it took. I needed medical information and I did not care if I had to visit Mary every week. I was not going to quit. After two premature births and the loss of one child, no one was going to deprive me of the information I sought. Once I even told Mary that I thought I had cancer and asked her to check to see if there was a history of cancer in my family. Oh course, that was confidential information and I was denied access.

To make matters worse, not long after Jeff was born my doctor informed me that I might need a hysterectomy. He stated that tests had revealed that there was a lot of damage and I may never be able to have more children. However, he was killed in auto accident before he could complete the medical tests and I chose not to pursue that area. I desperately wanted to have more children.

I remember one night when Jeff was two years old, that I cried myself to sleep. I had given up on my search. There were no new clues and I felt it was hopeless. So I grabbed the pink outfit that I received when I was pregnant for Jennifer and held it tight in my arms. It was all I had left of my little girl, other than the promise I made at the gravesite and that seemed impossible.

At that moment I became angry with God. I had always felt he did not give you more than you could handle. However, he may have judged me wrong. I was not the person he thought I was. I no longer had the strength to go on. All the doors in my search were closed. I felt isolated from my past and trapped in a future that I could not control.

When I finally fell asleep, sometime during that night I received another premonition. This time my dream displayed my birth parents divorce papers. I watched as the brightly lit papers floated towards me. I knew that it meant that there was a clue somewhere in the papers but we had combed them many times and found nothing.

When morning finally arrived I glanced at the papers again. I had always believed in my premonitions so I believed with all my heart the papers would reveal an important clue. Although my dream only displayed the divorce papers, I followed my instincts. Quickly I turned to the last page and there in big bold letters were two of my uncles' addresses. Although no one had ever seen that page before I was thankful I had it now.

It is hard describe the feelings I had inside as we searched for one of the addresses listed on the papers. As we approached the street, my stomach turned to knots and the anxiety of many years of guilt started to play on me. But yet I was overjoyed as we turned down the street. It was a moment I waited on for many years and now a lifetime of unanswered questions were just at my fingertips.

As we drove into the driveway I remember thinking what am I going to say? Nervously I walked to the door and knocked a couple of times before I saw the note. It simply read, *Bud, no longer lives here. Please do not leave his mail here*. Although I was disappointed because my uncle Bud had moved away I still believed that my premonition held the key to my long lost family.

We were not sure where the other address was, so we drove to the nearest gas station for directions. It seemed odd at the time but the attendant in the store would not allow female customers inside the building. So my husband Bob had to enter the store for directions and glance at the map. After several minutes of searching he was unable to locate the street. Several other men in the store had also tried to find it but were unsuccessful.

I think the appropriate thing to have done, would have been to drive to another gas station. However, my instincts would not let me walk away. Not even the devil could have stopped me. My faith had guided me here so I knew what I had to do. I entered the store and walked over to the map. Within seconds I had located the street. For some reason the street name stood out. Brightly lighted letters displayed the actual location of the street we were searching for.

Within moments we were on our way to the last address. It never entered my mind that he too could have moved. Again it wasn't long before I stood in front of a door that I had hoped would end the search for my long lost siblings. I knocked only once before a man approached. Oh God! He looks like father. As he patiently waited for a response my knees started to knock and I opened my mouth but the words did not come out. When I finally mustered enough strength I told him whom I was searching for. Before he replied, his wife approached the door. It was as if I was looking at my birth parents. I knew my uncle had asked a couple of questions but my heart beat so loudly that I simply could not hear him.

As they stood there looking at me with puzzled faces, I found myself wondering why they did not close the door. After all, I must have appeared crazy. Still they patiently waited for my response. Again he asked a question, "Who are you?" "My name is Kim," I said. I had not disclosed any more information other than my adoptive name when the people invited me into their home. As my husband and I entered the house my uncle asked, "Why are you looking for my brother?" I replied, "I am searching for my birth family. You were listed in my mother and father's divorce papers. I was hoping you could help me find my brothers and sister." "Are we the first people you found," He asked? So I told him about the other address of another uncle and his seemed surprised. Apparently his brother had moved many years ago and he thought it was odd that he would be still receiving mail.

After a brief conversation, I was informed that my father and his brother had married sisters, both my birth parents were still alive and someone had fought for custody of all seven of us kids. My Grandmother Vina had petitioned the court for legal guardianship for all of us. However, the court determined that due to her age it would be of our best interest that we be placed as permanent wards of the court. Shortly after that decision, she died of massive heart attack.

Less then two hours after my arrival I was calling my birth brother Allen. Because he was seventeen years old at the time of the family separation my aunt and uncle had taken him. Nervously I awaited a response on the other end of the phone. But the phone rang and rang. After what seemed eternity I heard a male's voice come to the phone and say, "This is Allen." I almost dropped the receiver.

I wasn't sure what to say so I stumbled over the words, "Allen this is Vina." For a moment the receiver went dead. Then I heard the brother that I hadn't talked to in thirteen years say, "Oh God! Where are you? When can I see you?" Holding back the tears I replied, "I can come over right now." Within minutes I was pulling into a driveway where a man was standing in the yard waiting impatiently.

It was like a dream come true. Standing by the brother I had lost so many years ago. For a moment time stood still and my tears erupted like a river running down steam. But I wasn't alone. He too had shed tears. This time they were tears of joy. We both had many questions about each other's lives and soon I was introduced to my sister in law and their three children.

Although father had forced Allen to drop out school many years ago, I was proud to hear that he had finished high school and held a good paying job. After we caught up on the small talk of where we were in our lives today he asked me if I wanted to talk to Betty. As Allen dialed her number I tried to think of all the questions I had rehearsed. But my mind went blank. While he waited for her to pick up the receiver he told me that she was expecting another child and that she was about nine months pregnant. After several minutes I watched as he started to hang up the phone. Oh God please let her answer. Then after a few seconds I heard my brother say, "Betty, you better sat down. I have some good news for you."

When Allen handed me the phone I could hardly talk. At first I didn't know what to say, she was a complete stranger. But somehow the bond we shared many years ago had carried to the present and within minutes I was talking to my long lost sister. At first we talked about our present lives and left the past alone. However, eventually we discussed the last moments of our lives as sisters and the effect it had on us. It seemed strange sharing that part of my life with someone but somehow I knew that she was one of the few people that truly understood the pain that I felt inside. As I listened to the pain of her youth, some of the pain I buried from my shattered childhood resurfaced. However this time it was comforting to know that at least three of us had survived.

Before the conversion was over I agreed to meet Betty, my brother Bob and father at her house. I could hardly believe that she lived just down the road from where I worked. After I hung up the phone, Allen told me that he would join all of us. However he asked me to pick up father because he had no room in his car and father did not drive. So I agreed. Although nervous about meeting father again I was assured that he had changed.

While driving to father's house my stomach turned to knots and my heart beat wildly. I desperately wished I had not agreed to pick him up. I just wasn't sure if I wanted him in my life right now and I wasn't sure how my adopted parents would feel about me seeing father again. They were the last people I wanted to hurt. They had spent years mending the damage father had done. How could I tell them I had looked him up?

Before I knew it I stood in front of the man called father. He seemed different. His frail body was nowhere near the size it had been so many years ago. His walk had slowed with age and now I no longer feared him. As he stood there waiting impatiently I knew he thought that I would ask a lot questions. But I didn't. Maybe in my youth I would have asked him why he treated his children so badly. But I no longer looked through the eyes of a child. The only question that came to my mind was, "If I had forgiven him sooner would this day have arrived sooner?"

When I arrived at Betty's house, my brother Bob and his wife were waiting to meet me. It seemed strange, the four of us together again. After a lot of tears and hugs we entered Betty's kitchen to talk.

Although all of our spouses were there, they remained in the living room with father. At first I listened to the echoes of my dreams. The same dreams that displayed the events of my of shattered childhood. For the last couple of years my husband had tried to explain to me that my mind might have made things worse than what they really were. It was comforting to hear that I was not crazy but that indeed my dreams played a major part of my childhood and I had not made them up.

Before the evening was over I had learned that they too had searched for me. However father had told them that I was placed in a mental institution many years ago and he thought I had not survived. However, they chose to search for me anyway. By placing an ad in the paper searching for a person named Vina they had actually found Tommy. Although he was still in high school and his adoptive family did not want us to have contact with him, we at least knew that he had survived. I would have given anything in the world to see him. I wanted to tell him how much I missed him and how sorry I was that I hadn't said good-bye. Maybe some day I'll be able to tell him but for now I would have to respect his adoptive family's decision.

It was comforting to hear that my brother Bob had seen Jim since the family separation however he was not sure where he was at this time. What was really strange, was the fact that both my brothers, Bob and Jim had attended school with my husband and all of us had graduated from the same high school. Also, Betty who graduated from a different school had actually lived in the area that my old classmates had seen someone that looked like my twin and when we looked at each other's graduation pictures we did look similar then. I guess it really is a small world. It amazes me to think that my birth siblings were right at my fingertips and I didn't even know it.

However, there were no clues as to where Chiefy was. Because of his age at the time of the family separation, we had to face the fact that he might be impossible to find. To make matters worse, he might not even remember us. I'll always remember the look in his eyes as he was taken from me. I'll never forget that promise I made to him. I'll find you little brother. I'll beat the odds! There has to be a way.

During the course of the evening I learned where my birth mother lived however I chose to wait to meet her. After meeting two brothers, Betty and father I had to deal with many buried memories and I just wasn't sure if I could handle any more. Besides it was nearly midnight and I was exhausted both emotionally and physically. When I finally decided to leave we promised to keep in touch and as I walked out of Betty's house I felt a sense of closure. Now for the first time in my life I was not burying my pain I was actually letting it out.

While we were driving home my husband apologized for not believing in the severity of the abuse that I endured. He told me that up until he heard a compete stranger tell the same story it was hard for him to believe that in this day and age something that terrible had actually taken place. Even more unbelievable was the fact that father had actually gotten away with it.

Father had never served one day in jail for the crime of child abuse. As a matter of fact, he had blamed my mother for everything. He simply said that he was innocent of all charges and somehow he had proved it in the court of law. What hurt the most was when he told me that he forgave me for lying to the judge. Perhaps someday I'll find out what happened in the courtroom and ask the judge why they let him go free.

Within a couple of hours of leaving my sister's house I was scheduled to work. Although I only had about two hours of sleep, I was not exhausted despite the fact that I had found it difficult to sleep. The morning hours went fast and before I knew it, it was noon. Already I was planning on meeting my sister after work and discussing our long lost years. Excitedly I told my boss about finding some of my birth siblings and he went into his usual lecture about his friend that had a terrible childhood and how he wanted to introduce us. I had heard about his friend many times over the last couple of years and I was not about to exchange horror stories about foster care. I was in search of my long lost siblings and that was what I was determined to concentrate on. Not a cook that worked with me a couple of years ago that had a rough childhood.

After work I went to Betty's house. We spent a lot of time together discussing the past and the present. It was easy to talk to her and we enjoyed catching up on all the years we missed. One day when I was at Betty's house we discussed how difficult it had been searching for each other. I even asked her if she had tried petitioning probate court. She only laughed. Apparently Betty's adoptive mother had worked for probate for many years and had been a transportation officer for both Tommy and me several times. Although she had told Betty that she seen us, she did not want us to find each other. Immediately I asked if her name was Mary and she stated Mary was one of her mother's friends. Betty also stated that she had petitioned the courts and felt that her petition went in the wastebasket. So I told her about how Mary treated me and made me feel like I was a criminal. However all the other doors were closed and I had no other place to find information other than our parents divorce papers. Betty immediately asked if she could have a copy but when I went to print her a copy, that last page was missing. Never to be found again.

We eventually introduced each other to our adoptive families. Although it was awkward at first, in my heart I now had two sisters, seven brothers, a mom and a dad. I guess it was my way of reassuring my adoptive family I still loved them. Although I never met my brothers' adoptive family we spent hours discussing our past and future. It seemed the bond we shared many years ago had lasted through the many years of separation.

Within a couple of months of finding some of my birth siblings I received a call. It was from a man claiming to be my brother Jim. Excitedly, I agreed to meet him at the restaurant where I worked. As every male customer entered I wondered whether he was my brother. Some of my co-workers even asked if the gay male who entered wearing a red dress and lipstick was my brother. It wouldn't have mattered. I loved my brother no matter how he turned out. I was not his judge; I was his sister.

By mid morning a gentleman entered the restaurant. Immediately my boss ran over to meet him. Before I knew it he was introducing me to his friend Jim. I'm not sure who was more surprised when we discovered his friend Jim was my brother. Although we did not have a lot of time to talk, I learned that my brother had joined the Army a few years back and was only here on a short leave. However, he had agreed to meet me at my house later that day.

When Jim arrived at my house he introduced me to his wife. I learned that he would soon be a father and chose to keep the subject on the present. Before the evening was over Jim turned to me and said that I brought back too many painful memories and I should understand why he could not see me. When he left he told my husband that he just could not deal with that part of his life. Although Jim promised to write on occasion he never gave me his address, nor did I ever receive a letter. I promised not to interfere in his life but maybe someday he'll choose to see me again.

As the months passed I shared many of my flashbacks with my birth siblings and somehow the pain that once accompanied them had diminished. Although the flashback of the watch bothered me just as much as if it was happening now, I at least had an outlet. It was then that I chose to pursue the outcome of the trial. However, once again I met with no success. It was confidential information and my name was changed. The person named Vina no longer existed.

To make matters worse I could not even obtain my medical records for the first ten years of my life. I have no proof that my birth name was Vina. All of her records had been sealed. I can remember being hospitalized a couple of times but I am not sure for what. However, I did find out that two other siblings were hospitalized at the same time. Their records were also sealed.

One day Betty and I went to the hospital closest to our old neighborhood and requested medical information from those years when we had lived with our birth parents. When the nurse asked for identification neither one of us had any id with our birth names. Both of our first names had been changed so we could not prove that we were Betty and Vina. Luckily when we explained the situation to the nurse on duty she was very understanding and had agreed to mail the information to us. Within a few days we both received a package in the mail from the hospital. We never told the nurse that she was the first person that actually helped us in our search. So we sent her flowers and a note that simply said, from the lost sisters.

I'm not sure how long it took me to call mother but when I finally did she was getting re-married. I had been invited to the wedding and I thought about going but I decided against it. For some reason her new husband had given me bad vibes and I always followed my instincts so I did not attend. However, a couple of months later I went to meet her. She was happy to see me. Gone were her long raven tresses, which were now short and gray. I watched her eyes as I approached the door. When I met her husband, he was very flirtatious so I chose to keep my distance.

About a year later I received another call from a brother. It was Tommy. God! I was happy to hear from him. We talked for hours. I remember one of the first things he asked of me was, why I hadn't said good-bye? I replied that it had been too painful. The truth was that in my heart, I just couldn't let go so I had promised to find him and I never gave up. I had wanted to shield him from the pain but couldn't. The courts took me away.

A few months later I met with Tommy. Words could not explain the feelings I had. It was truly a dream come true. After all those years it was I who had to look up at him, he was a grown man. Although at first I wondered whether it was truly Tommy, the moment I looked into his eyes I knew I found the brother I had been searching for.

Not long after that I gave birth to another son. During this pregnancy because of my tendency to deliver early, the doctor had me hospitalized the last couple weeks of my pregnancy. Just before I gave birth, my blood pressure shot up and the room filled with a strange darkness before I knew it, I was looking at my body. As I floated towards the door I could hear my doctor talking with another gentlemen. At first, as I listened to the conversation it appeared to be about a patient that was in serious condition. Although I did not know whom it was I prayed for, I hoped that they would make it.

Then suddenly an alarm sounded in a nearby room I watched as the doctor ran into my room. He started shaking me and I could hear him say, "Come back for the baby's sake!" As I re-entered my body, he wheeled me into the labor and delivery room where I gave birth to another son. It wasn't until the next day that my doctor told me that I had opened death's door. Although I could remember my out of body experience, I had felt that it was just one of my premonitions and never realized that I was near death. From that day on I realized that I had a special gift. Very few people have out of body experiences but those who do never forget them. After that I always followed my instincts.

Several weeks after I gave birth, I went to the doctor for my follow-up appointment. It was then that he told me what had occurred and that pre-eclampsia was a very serious condition that was rarely detected until the twenty eighth week of pregnancy. It was possible that during my first two pregnancies I had suffered from pre-eclampsia, which caused me to give birth prematurely. At least it was a medical answer for the loss of my daughter.

Five years later I gave birth to another son. I named him Thomas. Not after one person, but for the many. I couldn't find a more appropriate way to say thank you to the people that had made a difference in my life. Thank you.

By this time Chiefy would be almost twenty years old and I had no clues of his whereabouts. So one day Betty and I decided to attend an adoptee support group in a nearby town. They had listed an ad in the paper claiming to be able to obtain adoptee birth certificates. However, we were not children that were placed by private adoption agencies we were permanent wards of the court. We were the exception again.

By 1991 we heard that Mary retired from her probate court position. Immediately Betty and I went to Probate to petition for Chiefy. There standing behind the counter was a woman that greeted us with a warm friendly smile. After we filled out the forms she informed us that the cost had increased. At first we simply offered a check however they would only accept cash. Due to time constraints our only other option was to return the next day. I watched her as she played with the folders on the counter. The top one seemed to glow. Although she could not state the contents of the folder I knew that we had to obtain that folder. Unexpectedly someone setting in the room approached me and offered the difference. I turned and handed the money to woman at the counter. I quietly completed all paperwork but when I turned to thank our benefactor, he had left.

Because we only had enough money for one of us to petition Betty received the call the next day. It was from probate court. Chiefy had an active file petitioning for his birth family. However, Chiefy lived out of state. So a time was set up for him to call. Because we could not see each other it made it more difficult. The first thought that entered my mind was "How do I know that this is my brother?" So we asked a lot of questions. What he looked like? What he remembered? Then we asked about his eye. There was a burn mark on his eyelid but he could see perfectly. He had one question for us, what is a Chiefy?

During the summer months Chiefy made the trip to Michigan with his wife and children. After twenty-three years six out of the seven of us were re-united. Our search was over. The little brother that was forcibly removed from my arms was now standing in front of me. The first thing I said was "I'M SORRY." I had always blamed myself for losing him. Yet as he hugged me tightly he simply replied, "I remember you." It was then that I whispered, "I kept my promise Chiefy, you're home."

In 1993 Allen, Betty, Chiefy and myself petitioned probate for the trial records. This is the outcome. My parents, plea bargained down to a neglect charge and received no time in jail. They were found guilty of not having enough food, shampoo and cleaning supplies, mother was charged with having sexual intercourse with one of her sons. Betty was described as being an extremely bright child whose insight appeared greatly in excess of her age. The three oldest children passed the polygraph test. Father was found deceptive.

My testimony and medical tests were gone. Expunged from the files due to the number of years that had passed by. All birth certificates are sealed. Permanent wards of the court are never granted access although the private sector adoptions can obtain their records. As for my search, four of our first names were changed and so was one birthday. We also discovered that Chiefy's file had been pulled because he was being reclassified in the service. If we had waited until the next day our files would have not been placed together. It would have been on someone's desk to be filed. It was at this time the picture I had taken of Tommy and I was returned to me. Betty's mother had been able to obtain the picture from the files before they were expunged.

In 1993 father died of lung cancer he left behind many unanswered questions. So my search goes on. As for Jimmy I'm still waiting and hoping that someday the seven of us will be re-united once again. Perhaps someday all of us will close the eyes of a child we once were and forget the past.

# Epilogue

It is now springtime 2003 the end of my trail. I've reached my summit and I set my pen aside to reflect. The Cherokee people have a purification ritual called, "going to the water." Has this book been my cleansing of the soul? During the past several months, I have opened many doors and looked deep within myself. There have been many tears shed during the setting down of words to this story. A story I've wanted to tell since I was that little nine-year old girl. This story unfortunately, even to this day, continues to be acted out only too frequently. I've discovered that there is life after the storms. Wounds will heal and something beautiful can be nurtured, coached into brilliance.

I think it was William Shakespeare who wrote the following line in, *JULIUS CAESAR,* "Mans fate is not in the stars but in themselves." Despite the horrors of my youth, I find myself surrounded by my boys and my family. I have my health, I'm professionally employed and I've completed a dream. I have survived and conquered the challenges of my past. My birth siblings have also weathered their storms. They may be found in the ranks of the clergy, nursing and military professions.

I read with interest the newspaper articles pertaining to crimes committed against children and I'm still appalled by them and wonder what drives the parents and family members to perpetrate such heinous crimes against their own flesh and blood. One cannot help but notice the laws governing the reporting of abuse, that now exist. The organizations developed to assist the victims with overcoming their fears and placing them into a more secure loving environment. Are there still cracks through which one might fall? Yes! That will always exist in a bureaucracy. However, had this system been in place in the 1960s would those agonies I had to suffer been foreshortened?

It is my sincere hope that this book will provide some inspiration and a degree of solace for those unfortunate people who have suffered under similar circumstances. Should anybody find herself or himself for that matter currently undergoing these horrors, PLEASE SEEK HELP! You are a human being with rights under the law. Seek the guidance of your clergy, a school counselor or your family physician. Tell another family member, whose trust you value. Look in the phone book for crisis intervention centers and of course report the abuse to the law enforcement agencies. DO NOT listen to your abuser, you are not deserving of the cruelties being forced upon you. Remember YOU ARE A VICTIM!

There have been times during the writing of my story, that I've found myself wondering if I was actually doing the writing. Throughout my book, you have read of my visions and the presence of my Grandfather's spirit. Is it tobacco, I think I smell even now as I type? Does he still continue as a friendly overseer in my life? I know what I believe and I thank-you Grandfather. Has my gift of sight been passed down to my sons? Only recently has my middle son made reference to strange feelings and visitations by unknown personages. Has his great grandfather made his presence known? My youngest son seems susceptible to my awareness of the supernatural. I have a niece whom has demonstrated an uncanny receptivity to visions. Perhaps only in the future will it be shown if these special gifts manifest themselves in my sons.

Within the story you heard me use the terms mother, father, mom and dad. These terms were not used interchangeably. My sons have been taught from an early age to address me as mom or mommy, never as mother. Mother and father are terms I gave to the people who bore me. They were only responsible for my biological existence. Mom and dad are my adoptive parents. These are the real parents who nurtured and bestowed their love upon me. They are responsible for the woman I have become.

My grandma Jo died in Arizona but not before I had climbed that mountain in the Superstitions where her ashes now repose. After her death I found her *last dollar*, still folded after all these years.

An author in their acknowledgements lists the people who have played a significant role in the success of their book. At this time I would like to offer my sincere thanks to you the reader, who spent both your time and money to listen to my story, it is one thing to be a published author, it is quite another to be one that is read. Thank-you!

K. S. Thomas
Saginaw Bay, MI